ISH VERDUZCO

HOW SUCCESSFUL PEOPLE GET ISH DONE

A 7-STEP FRAMEWORK
TO ACHIEVE YOUR GOALS

Copyright © 2020 Ish Verduzco

This book is sold subject to the condition that it shall not, by way of trade or otherwise, be lent, resold, hired out, or otherwise circulated without the publisher's or author's consent.

All rights reserved.

ISBN: 9798646094330

Images in this book are also the intellectual property of Ish Verduzco.

Graphic Design & Credits: Ish Verduzco, Freepik.

HOW SUCCESSFUL PEOPLE
GET ISH DONE

*"If you can't fly, then run.
If you can't run, then walk.
If you can't walk, then crawl.
But whatever you do, you have to keep moving forward."*

Martin Luther King Jr.

Dedicated to:
Ismael Verduzco Jr.
Jose Verduzco
Joseph Justin Phan
Lucas Adrian Gutierrez

If you find any value from this book,
please share it with your friends and family.
They also deserve the knowledge to achieve their goals.

Ish Verduzco

Content

13	**A Head's Up: Warnings of What's to Come**
21	**Prologue**
24	Why Did I Write This Book?
30	So, Why Did I Write It?
31	Why Would You Believe Me?
32	What Is My Method Based On?
34	What Am I Buying?
37	**Chapter 1: You**
40	Understanding What Self-Aware Means
42	Self-Concept
50	The You Test
53	Ish Under the Microscope
54	Ish Under the Microscope, Part 2
59	**Chapter 2: Game Changers**
60	What is an Algorithm?
63	Habits, Rituals, and Routines
69	Habits
72	Creating a Habit
79	How to Build a Good Habit
83	How Do I Break a Bad Habit?
86	Rituals
89	Rituals of Successful People
89	Questions to Ask Yourself
92	Ish's Rituals

93	**Chapter 3: Learning Square**
96	Books, Books, and More Books
97	Art, Education, and Brain Chemistry
99	The Tree of Knowledge: Hollywood Edition
101	Compound Learning
104	"What Makes MJ, well, MJ?"
107	The 25-Minute Hack
109	**Chapter 4: Putting in the Work**
114	The Genetical Breaking Point
115	"You Should Be Gettin' It…"
116	Time Is On Your Side
122	21st Century Dynamics
125	Putting It All Together
127	The Mayer Dynamic
131	**Chapter 5: You got one hell of an Ego**
135	You Deluded F&%K
136	The Science of Self-Delusion
138	Confidence is King
139	Ego is Queen
141	Be Batman
143	The Science of the Dark Knight
145	The Value of Self Talk
149	Ish's Affirmations

151	**Chapter 6: Eyes on the price**
152	The Reality of Goals
155	The Fatalist Feature
160	Creating Your Own Luck
166	Instinct, Luck, or Something Else?
170	SMART Goals
175	**Chapter 7: The Yoda Model**
176	The Monomyth
179	Meeting the Mentor
181	The Mentor Mentality
183	The Importance of a Mentor
185	Finding a Mentor
185	Friends & Family
189	**Chapter 8: Bringing it all together**
189	Between a Rock and a Hard Place
191	Let's Crunch the Numbers
193	A Writer's Workshop
200	The Hypothetical Hippodrome
209	**Afterword: What It All Means**
215	**A Note from the Author**

A Head's Up
Warnings of What's to Come

This book is really the first thing I've actually written with any sort of passion and foresight. I'm not exactly known for my way with words. Halfway into the process, I slipped into a reflective mode, reading and hatching away at every passage, article, word, and section. Doubting absolutely everything. Edits, rewrites, deletes. The equivalent of balls of crumbled yellow Post-It notes tossed at a wall. Piles and mountains of them. I wanted the book to start off with a bang. Something that would seize the audience's attention and put into perspective what was at stake. A real, honest-to-God reflection of success and triumph. For months, the following placeholder catapulted this book into action:

[Insert Inspirational Tale. Mike? Kobe? Jobs? Barack?]

No, that's not a typo. I literally had that there because I wanted to kick off the book with an inspirational tale that would grab your attention as a reader. Something that would really set the stage. As I went on and wrote the rest of the book, this section haunted me. It dogged my heels, not because it was impossible to truly drag out an eloquent and gripping, sometimes even stunning, story of one of those amazing people surpassing insurmountable odds, but because after a while, although they still managed to inspire me, their tales didn't exactly click with the way the book was turning out. They enticed and encouraged, they influenced and moved, they roused and motivated, but the way I was analyzing them felt hollow. Let me explain.

These paragons are the yardstick by which we measure success. They are the mirror image of what we want to be. They, and a thousand others, are the stories of what it means to be authentic and not only follow your dreams but obtain them. Each one of their hard-earned lessons needs to be dissected and examined…but they are still very much flawed creatures. Why? Because to err is human[1]. As I dug deeper into this book, I began to understand a bit about myself. I began to reflect on the lessons I had learned, the lessons I will teach you, and the lessons they had taught me. I began to understand how certain beliefs and dogmas shaped the person I am today, and how other exercises simply clashed against the reality of who I am. This book, as it turned out, was as much as an exploration of who I am as a symposium of what I've got to say. The deeper I fell down the rabbit hole, the more I challenged my beliefs, and the greater insight I acquired.

As I neared the end of the book, I realized that it was shaping me as much as I was shaping it. It was making me reevaluate what I knew, concentrate on what mattered, and take a step back and truly observe who I had become. So, I went back to the beginning and read that line over and over again:

"Insert Inspirational Tale. Mike? Kobe? Jobs? Barack?"

---

[1] To make grand errors is human. We all make errors and stumble along the way; it's part of the whole human existence. Oscar Wilde - because frankly if you're out of quotes and want a really good one, you can always unearth one of his nuggets. He once said, *"If you're not making errors, then you're simply not living."*

Each and every one of the successful people that I studied will have their say in this book, but I certainly couldn't start with one of their stories...mainly because their stories weren't mine. I can begin to know the way President Obama's father's abandonment truly shaped him. I could reread the transcripts. I could examine his interpretations. I could delve deep into his biography, but that moment - way back in his childhood - when he finally understood what had occurred and he started to grapple with that loss, was gone. I was getting third-hand knowledge and, above all, a personal narrative that had been dulled by time and shaped by politics. I wasn't getting the emotional rawness of that kid, I was getting the savvy, mature, and spin-doctor analysis of the President. I was getting the brand and the shaped story, not the reality. The reality, that moment, had been doctored and photoshopped.

As humans, we have an amazing ability to re-tell history, particularly our own. It's something innate and something we don't do consciously. We have an identity and that identity is intently tied to the narrative we want to show and we want to believe in. We're nothing more than what we show the public. When something from our present, which will soon become our past, strikes a discordant note with that ideal, we go into triage. We wax, we edit, we color, we smooth it. We do this process until we've told the new version of that event, painted by our own biases, so frequently that we no longer recall the actuality of what happened...just the story. Our Hollywood-edited version.

Sociologists call this "Narrative Bias" or "Narrative Fallacy." In short, it refers to a person's tendency to interpret information as being part of a larger story or pattern, regardless of whether the facts support the full narrative. It is something that is done at an unconscious level.

This is something we have always fallen victim to. It comes naturally to us. As humans, we don't deal with numbers, stats, or facts; we deal with emotions. We are sold the idea of a cause and are rarely moved by the numbers and figures; instead, we donate to the example - the individual heart-rending tale. We don't donate to the plight of the millions of refugees, but the struggles of the poster child. This is because as humans, we're not that adept at facing the truth. The truth hurts and in many cases, it goes against the idea of who we are. We don't like figures, we like tales. The truth is harsh. So, when we're faced with a truth that causes us pain, regret, or shame, we start to mold it until it barely resembles its former self. We craft it into something perceptible that adheres to our identity. This bias, with which we later retell our tales, is something common in all of us. It's something we always do. We do it to such an extreme that, thanks to technology, we are now outsourcing it. We no longer have to rely on what we tell but what our onscreen persona displays. Or are you the person you purport to be on Facebook?

A great example of this inherent quality can be found in our social media feeds. Look back at your feed – is it real? Do those pictures tell the whole story? You seem like the perfect couple, everyone marveling at both your chiseled bodies and your interactions, but do those pictures and stories tell the whole tale? Do your friends and audience members know of the constant bickering? Or that maybe you were faking that smile because a second ago you had been in an argument? Do they know that your family holiday was plagued by traffic, family squabbles, your parents' constant criticizing, the fact that the turkey gave you a stomach ache, that you had to sleep in an uncomfortable pull-out couch, that your cousin got hammered and made a fool of himself? No, you CHOSE the perfect pic, and that one pic will in time become the memory of that Thanksgiving dinner. Over time, that personage you sell overrides the truth. In a year or two, you'll look at that photo and gloss over all the turmoil and unhappiness and remember only the good times. You're telling a story and that story is you.

We all do this. I'm as guilty as you – just look at my feed on Instagram. And Mike, Kobe, Jobs, Barack, all their feeds - books, social presence, articles - were cherrypicked and worked by experts. They tell their version. Not so much what they want you to know but what clicks with their brand. Is it a false story? No. Not in the least. It's simply a story that adheres to the narrative; the narrative they have devised and the narrative we have linked them with.

Those constructs and archetypes are only reinforced through each retelling, the legend or ensemble no longer built on the facts, but on the idea promoted on the moral. Each anecdote lined with meaning. Each true-life story slowly becoming a parable and transforming into a fable; a fairytale. Those historical events slowly morph into oral traditions, children's stories with simple themes, and moral certitudes that slip into the collective subconscious. The human condition examined in simple sound bytes. Haven't you noticed that Twitter, Facebook, Snapchat, and all other forms of digital social interactions are based on an allegory or a story to teach? When you go online, to be successful, you have to sell an idea: yours or someone else's. Successful people, after a while, cultivate that paradigm; every story they have, every tale they tell, lined with meaning; part of their legend. Meaning and symbolism they ascribe after careful edits and after it has been tested on focus groups.

They do this under the same care we do it. There's no ill intent, there are no ulterior motives, it's simply how we are constructed. It's how we communicate with one another, not through facts but stories. *The Origin Of Species* by

Darwin might be a great book, but as a race, we find more significance and are influenced more profoundly by *Star Wars*. Evolution and natural selection, the building blocks of life, coming in a third or fourth place to Jedi Knights and Sith Lords.

So, I really can't tell you what psychological torment or shifting dynamics Obama's personality endured during those bygone days of parental woes. I can't properly convey the bodily trials endured by Kobe during his training, let alone the emotional merry-go-rounds he had to live through every single day. I can't do justice to them, and to you, because I'm only reading their Facebook feeds. I'm only dissecting their biographies, their after-action reports, their mythical construction.

As I said, I can't lecture on what pre-teen Obama felt on that day...but I can talk about how I felt the day my father died. I can't talk about Kobe's sacrifices every morning, but I can tell you about my routines and how they've helped shape me into the man that I am today. I can use their framework, their folklore, and their "once upon a time" to better understand my own stories. To better comprehend my struggles. To rework my tales from the ground up.

Once more I'm met with that phrase:

[Insert Inspirational Tale. Mike? Kobe? Jobs? Barack?]

And I think, now that the book is almost finished, that it was the wrong Post-It/ reminder for so many reasons. I should, first and foremost, talk about myself. This is not an attempt at legend building or self-adulation; I'm as screwed up as the next guy. Why? Because, honestly, I'm not perfect. I've had a ton of downfalls just like anyone else. I have some triumph and victories, but for every "atta boy" on social media, I have had a thousand more fumbles and times where it seemed like my life was falling to pieces.

My name is Ish Verduzco and I'm a proud Latino from Los Angeles, California. A first-generation college grad from very humble beginnings. Extremely confident in my ability to achieve anything that I set my mind to, but still struggling with self-doubt and imposter syndrome at times. Addicted to learning, growing, and pushing myself to be a better version of myself each and every day, yet I still floundered in most of my classes from elementary school to university. A DJ, a Podcaster, a former Athlete, an Entrepreneur, a Marketer, and now, an Author.

This is as much my tale, as it is Obama's, Beyonce's, Oprah's, the Rock's, Kobe's, Michael's, Jobs', and dozens more…but, more importantly, it is yours.

Prologue

Great, you're here. Pat yourself on the back, crack open a Modelo, or pour yourself a cup of Joe, and let's get this party started. I was 23 when this whole journey began. This obsessive desire for learning was triggered by Shane Snow's phenomenal book *Smartcuts: How Hackers, Innovators, and Icons Accelerate Success*. Before plowing through this book multiple times, I wasn't a reader by any standard. I actually hated reading. Somehow Shane's book managed to hook me. It changed the way I think about achieving goals. His concept of lateral thinking blew my mind.

> *"The fastest route to success is never traditional, and the conventions we grew up with can be hacked."*

We live in a world completely different from that of our parents. That's the first thing you have to understand. The conventions and ideals of them can't be applied to modernity. Every sphere of interaction right now, from relationships to business dynamics, is utterly different from the pillars that kept our parents' paradigm stable. Our educational system's approach is still stuck in the mindset of yesteryears, in the way things were done while our parents learned the multiplication table and recited the elements; flooding us with data and information, treating us as a repository, and neglecting our capacity to process. With smartphones at our fingertips and the world - not to mention Wikipedia at our beck and call - we are still being taught multiplication tables and important dates in American history; facts and data that we can call up with a simple, "Hey, Alexa..."

We have outsourced our capacity to store information and now we should be instrumented on how to process and analyze it. How to interact, digest, and comprehend the endless streams of data coming our way.

Our parents grew up in a world where the paradigm was set in stone after the Industrial Revolution - you got a job, you paid your dues, you got married, you climbed the ladder, you had kids, you retired. The new generation is evolving amidst the birthing pains of the Digital Revolution. We have to face the shifts of Big Data, the leaps of AI, the power of globalization and Instant Message, the struggle of machine learning, and automatization. We live in a world of lateral thinking. In the world of UBER instead of taxis. In the world of Airbnb instead of Hilton. In the world of Zoom calls instead of 12-hour airplane rides and board meetings. Our jobs are at the mercy of technology; what we learned at the university might be challenged by AI within a few years. Our posts might become irrelevant due to a new program. We might have to constantly reinvent ourselves. We no longer have to pay our dues and put in the time; one good idea, one revolutionary, though, might spring us to the top. Married? Why? Thanks to safe sex policies and pansexual practices, we're no longer bound by established norms. We don't have to give birth at a young age because we're now in control of our biological clock…and even if it starts to falter along the way, we can always adopt or try in-vitro fertilization. Thanks to modernity, we can now live 20% longer than our parents…there isn't a need to retire at 60 or 70.

We are the children of a world where sexuality is up for debate and our parents' standard careers no longer exist, and every second new job flowers into existence. We live in a new dawn, a world that can be hacked, a world governed by Google, social media, and Apple…not a world of 9 to 5.

We live in an age where reinventing yourself is no longer seen as something odd…it's the norm.

This is no longer our parents' or our grandparents' past. It's a world where what really matters, what is really valuable, isn't gold, land, or tangible objects but ideas. China can't invade Silicon Valley because it can't mine the riches being produced there. It can't storm the latest tech start-up because all it will find and manage to take is a building brimming with computers… The true value of what was being produced there, the technicians and masterminds, on Gulfstream Jets high over the Rocky Mountains. In one day, China makes more money in trade deals with Silicon Valley than the yearly sum of profit the Congo makes off diamonds.

We have to think lateral, outside the box, and above all, outside our parents' norm.

Let's get something straight – the last thing I want to do is mislead you and quite possibly deceive you. Cruising down the Amazon aisle, fretting on where to drop your hard-earned cash, juggling between a bit of self-improvement and maybe a science fiction novel, you somehow stumbled onto this book and maybe a little voice inside your head went:

> *"Hmmmm. It sounds good. I wanna get shit done. I wanna be successful. I wanna achieve my goals. So what am I holding back on?! Take my money and let's get this show on the road!"*

Well, however you came upon this book, the important fact is that you CAME UPON it. And more notably - considering the ADHD culture we live in - that you're taking the time to read it. Kudos to you. That's something to tweet about. Done? Ok, now let's dig in…

Why Did I Write This Book?

I've got to be upfront and honest with you – this is not like most self-help books you've read. This is not a humanitarian, "you are the best, you go champ, you got this" type of book. If it makes you happy, you are a superstar and you can accomplish anything. There, now that we got that out of the way, let's move on to the next topic.

Next, I'm no one's guru.

Why?

Because I understand two things and those two fundamental things are partly what inspired me to write this book.

The first critical one has to do with the greatest scientific discovery of history, the one thing that inspired the likes of Newton, Einstein, and Currie. The one fundamental factor that was pivotal to the development of mankind and our ability to unshackle ourselves from the obscure thinking of the Dark Ages. What did science uncover? Science discovered ignorance. Up until that moment - where we as a species realized that we simply didn't know - the wheels of progress had been hindered by our excessive pride. In other words, by the fact that we thought that we knew best, that we knew absolutely everything, and for the mysteries of life we had the Bible, the Torah, the Quran, or some other religious book to tell us what to do. If it wasn't in some religious book, then not only was it not true, but it fell outside our scope; we really didn't need to know. If the Bible didn't tell us why the sky was blue, then, simply put, God didn't want us to know, so why bother? If the Torah didn't specifically give us the

4-1-1 on what those blinking lights up in the night sky were, then we really shouldn't be asking.

Columbus crashed like a drunken fool into a new continent based on the fact that scientifically, not religiously, he thought he might reach India; up until that point everyone was certain that the world was flat…and because our religious books and our religious scholars didn't contradict that notion, then it was a certainty. For a few years, humanity was being chased by these old beliefs, driven by ignorance and passionate understanding that the Church knew best. The people in charge yelling, "Will you just accept it?" And "If you get too uppity, then we'll burn you as a witch." To put it in terms you can relate to, imagine that back in the 60s, when science was 100% certain of its space program, then midway through the Apollo 11 mission, Armstrong uncovers a planet hidden between the moon and Earth.

The world, in that era, collectively said to themselves…

> *"Shit, we know nothing!"*

Or think about how dumbfounded the people in the late 1800s must've been when they discovered that they could speak with their friends and relatives through the first telephone. They probably said to themselves…

> *"And we thought those telegraphs were the best form of communication. We really know nothing!"*

Now, all of these examples top of mind, we as a species understood the value of ignorance. It wasn't something to be ashamed of but rather the excitement and curiosity that inspires change and exploration. And as we continued to recognize its potential, we uncovered that each new observation, every new busted myth, and each new invention equipped us with POWER. In understanding how antibiotics work and, for that matter, uncovering the existence of viruses and bacteria, we beat back Pestilence and Plague. In comprehending weather patterns, soil samples, and later on, genome therapy and how to apply it to agriculture, we no longer lived in extreme scarcity of food availability. In realizing the power of the atom - installing the MAD (Mutually Assured Destruction) doctrine - and then promoting diplomatic relationships between states, we gave War a break.

Our ignorance and embrace of it drove us to enlightenment. And we still know NOTHING. Today's reveal might be tomorrow's improvement…as it has happened so many times in the past.

So, that's the first thing you have to comprehend. We know nothing. The faster we are able to accept that, the faster we are to learning.

This book itself is simply a tool that I'm using to coherently summarize everything I've studied and absorbed.
Maybe I struck gold. Maybe I've stumbled onto a secret formula… Or, just maybe, I have no idea what I'm talking about and just wasted a good chunk of my life writing this book... But, then again, isn't that what life is all about? Trying things, testing, pressing boundaries, learning, growing, and following that curiosity inside each and every one of us.

So, here's the first confession. I'm as ignorant as you are. The only difference is that I read up on it for nearly a thousand hours and now have a book to show what I've learned.

That's the first thing. Part one of the two-part saga as to why I wrote this book. The second concern has to do with those prolific slogans.

"Just Do It!"
"Live Free and Die Hard!"
"Think Differently."
"Because you're worth it!"

Thousands of taglines and quotes meant to uplift us and make us feel like we are precious commodities.

Thousands of ad campaigns, our family, our teachers, and society as a whole continuously tell us one consistent motto:

"You're awesome and you can do it!"

But there's always the one key ingredient they seem to lack…

The HOW.

Whenever I read those uplifting, marketing-tweaked buzzwords and heavy calls to action, I'm reminded of the missing piece of the puzzle that they constantly fail to include: the "how." It seems as though this is always sidestepped. They paint the pretty picture that you can go from point A to point Z seamlessly, while skipping everything in between.

Here's an illustration to bring help you wrap your mind around the point.

Imagine you're back in school, you look out the window, and see a grey cloud right outside. Then, Flash! A thunderstorm breaks and suddenly it's raining cats and dogs. You raise your arm and ask:

"Teacher, why is it raining?"

The teacher turns to you and glares. "Because it was cloudy just a second ago. Can't you see that? Now stop asking rhetorical questions."

Phase One: It's cloudy.
Phase Two: ?
Phase Three: It's raining.

You're missing the most crucial ingredient. The math that turns One to Three. You got an equation but you're missing a variable to complete the equation.

It's like saying:

Pink elephant + $X = 42$.

There's no way to of knowing what X means in relationship to the pink elephant unless you did research and found the correlation between the two. The same goes for the question you asked your teacher. The only way to know why it's raining is by going to the library and diving into the scientific data.

That same algorithm can be applied to almost all the mottos, and phrases that you find in all of those "motivational" Instagram captions.

Grab any off the internet and you're faced with an encouraging but ultimately hollow message.

> *"It's always the simple that produces the marvelous."*

So, how do I produce the simple? What is marvelous? How do I get to any of these two points? What if I created something simple and it sucks?

> *"The pessimist sees the difficulty in every opportunity.*
> *The optimist sees opportunity in every difficulty."*

Great, finally, a starting point. A simple, clear path to follow. Only now you're missing the key ingredient and the one thing even Churchill didn't know how to quantify. How do I become an optimist?

Now, as a final example, let's look at Nike's famous product-selling catchphrase:

> *"Just Do It!"*

Ask yourself the following:

Just do what? How do I do it? It just seems to accentuate a feeling of haste and speed, so, how do I do that mysterious "It"?

Phase One: You are the best. You can do anything. You are Rocky!
Phase Two: ?
Phase Three: Buy that Porsche, and while you're at it, think like Scarface and decorate your garden with a tiger or two.

When I started down this rabbit hole, I quickly came to the realization that we are missing Phase Two.

We're missing the "How" successful people get shit done.

So, Why Did I Write It?

First, because I believe that more people deserve to have the knowledge and resources to achieve their goals. It shouldn't solely be for the educated, wealthy, or average person who indulges in the countless self-development books on a regular basis.

Second, because I want show people from underrepresented groups that it is possible for them to achieve their goals, even when sometimes there aren't people who look like them, talk like them, or come from similar backgrounds as they do in those fields.

But whether you were born with a silver spoon or not, sometimes we just need someone to give us a hand and help us out. And I'm hoping that I can be that person to provide a lending hand.

Moving on to next part of why I wrote this book.

Have you ever wondered how some people manage to have all their ducks in a row all the time? Why some people continuously fountain success while others try to break the glass ceiling with their forehead? Why some people always seem to be on a natural high? Why some are so energetic, motivated, and relentless, and seem like they have life all figured out?

Well, I did. And those are some of the burning questions that drove me to write this book.

And through my 930 hours of research, I learned that all of those wildly successful people focus most of their energy on one thing.

They focus on THE HOW.

Why Would You Believe Me?

You don't have to. I'm just a guy with a theory and a path that worked for ME. But I've pressure-tested this theory with countless of the world's most successful people. Now it's your turn to use your life and experiences as your personal science experiment to prove that this theory works.

This is a win-win situation. If my guide passes the test, then you're better off... and me, I'll be helping millions of people around the world, while giving the lady who wrote *Harry Potter* a run for her money. If, on the other hand, my hypothesis flops, then all you lost are a couple of bucks and a quick read. You're back to square one.

But actually on second thought, you're not. Even if my experiment flops, you will have changed a bit. How? Because I'm confident that this experience will have taught you something new. We grow and mature based on a feedback loop between experience and sensibility. Our brain makes new neurons and synaptic pathways based on the experiences we undertake. In turn, these brainy electrical jolts and synaptic routes tweak our sensibility levels.

Our sensibility levels are what we use to emotionally digest, catalog, and analyze experiences. The more we see, do, and hear, the better our understanding of ourselves and the world around us. A feedback loop: the more experiences, the better your sensibility levels…the better you sensibility levels, the greater degree you have of properly addressing and analyzing your future experiences.

So, even if I don't make a multimillionaire out of you, I can scientifically prove - without a shadow of a doubt - that you will be a different person after you read this book and perform the exercises in it.

And, what If my method works? Then, you'll find yourself smashing through lists of goals that you never thought you'd get to.

What Is My Method Based On?

A couple of years ago I slipped into an obsession of learning about how the world's most successful people had gotten to where they are or were during the peak of their careers. At the time, I didn't think to write a book; I honestly just wanted to learn as much as possible so that I could find key themes and apply the knowledge to my life, then share whatever worked with my close friends and family.

I jumped in and researched over 400 interviews, 35 books, 20 documentaries, and countless research studies. Over five years of learning and amassing quantifiable data on what makes some of the world's biggest tech companies tick... Not just an in-depth investigation of modern companies and their CEOs, but on the lives of people like Rockefeller and Flagler, too.

The smartest people, the lucky few, the terminally obsessive, even the Morgan Freemans of the industry...I studied all of them. Their speech patterns, their follies, their media screw-ups, their setbacks, their triumphs, their upbringing, and everything in between.

After thousands of rinse-and-repeat moments and getting tossed off the horse, all these people had many commonalities. Determining characteristics that either came innately to them, or they slowly developed through trial and error. Let me make something very clear: These tactics were not tied to genetics, socioeconomic status, race, gender, or industry. Sure, shooting out of a well-to-do womb and landing in a place where the silver spoon has been replaced by a gold one helps, but most of the underdogs I studied were just that: underdogs.

Sure, you can have a genetic prowess like Marvin Gaye: a voice blessed by biology... But most musicians and singers were taught how to harmonize, and vocalize. Beyonce, Presley, Jackson, Mana, Sinatra, Prince – they all did the work and followed a common equation.

This book has synthesized over 930 hours of research on the subject. Taken away all the fat, filtered out the minutiae, dug a grave for the exemptions, and focused on the framework. On clearly outlining a 7-step strategy on how to get shit done.

What Am I Buying?

I'm not here to drag on and on about the characteristics of successful people. A quick Google search basically tells you that successful people are unicorns. Optimistic, determined, relentless, passionate, and disciplined people that pretty much poop rainbows and butterflies. They are supposed to be mythical creatures with biological and chemical makeups that make them our psychological superiors.

If you want quick tips on how to transform into this representation of Google's gauge and indicator for potential success, then, by all means, use the search engine and do a quick recon of what it offers. But if that's all the effort you are willing to put in, be sure to hand this book over to someone with real success on their mind. I don't offer platitudes and empty cheers; I offer exercises vetted by academics and not Instagram celebs – by psychologists, neurologists, and people who changed the world.

This is a book that tells you how to be fortunate and fruitful in your lane. It is meant to give you a blueprint on how to, if not beat the system, understand how the system functions and to comprehend that you can actually work within it.

What you're buying:

- A 7-step framework for success
- Tons of synthesized research
- Moments where you know I sat down with a beer after hitting the wall that they call "writer's block"
- No B.S. tactics
- Inspirational stories that will get you up off your ass and moving
- Moments when I was drinking a strong cold brew at one of the many overpriced coffee shops in LA, thinking to myself, 'Damn, I'm really writing a book. Who do I think I am?? The same guy that voluntarily only read about two books up until the age of 23. And I think I'm qualified to write one?!'

More than a book, I'm offering you an experience. Make sure to put on your seatbelt as you jump in my spaceship and I'll take us on a journey that you needed but didn't know you wanted.

1
YOU

"Let go of who you think you're supposed to be; embrace who you are."

Brené Brown

OK, get ready, because we are about to go deep. We're going to explore not only the idea of YOU, from the purely philosophical point of view but, with that definition up for grabs, the neurobiological basis of identity. And, more importantly, why it matters and why you should embrace it.

Self-awareness is a tricky subject. The idea of a "self" and "us" concurrently using our perceptions to identify and quite possibly quantify reality seems a bit iffy. Why? Because it's sort of like using a tool you engineered from a mysterious compound to analyze said compound. We're supposed to employ our perception and our consciousness to identify and come to terms with our identity…which is basically constructed by our perceptions and our consciousness.

Let's take into account the following mental game and do a few brainy gymnastics:

A face appears in the sky. A man with one eyeglass that kinda looks like the guy from Monopoly. He rasps, coughs a bit and, while you're still in shell-shock and half the nuclear arsenal in the world is pointing at this visage, he says:

> *"Well, hey… Here's the scoop."* He waves his arms about encompassing the globe. *"This has been a huge - and I mean - HUGE experiment to understand character, feelings, actions, desires, and motivations of the self. Here's the thing, you're all real…what isn't real is this reality."*

The President goes crazy and presses the big, flashing, red button. BOOM. It's on now.

"That won't do," the malicious Monopoly man exclaims as he snaps his fingers and nuclear warheads turn into Skittles.

> *"Now where was I? Yes, reality is a sham...and you all signed NDA forms so you can't sue. A couple of years back, we hooked humanity up in a virtual reality simulator. Linked you up with science. And we gave one of you, just one, a subconscious control over the simulation. This VR playground is built on their experiences and their perceptions..."*

> *"...So, my question is, and then we can reboot the experiment and get you off the Matrix, which of you is it?"*

See, how can you judge that's you? How can you be certain that all you've experienced and sensed and analyze is the real reality and not your neighbor's or your co-worker's or your brother's or, for that matter, the bus driver's? You're self-aware, you're real, you're sure of it... But - and here's the question - if you only have YOU as a litmus test for YOU, then how can YOU be certain of the results?

Your brain hurts, right? Too much in too little time. I'm making you question the world around you.

But, does it matter? Let's say the world really is a VR playground and, for that matter, you're not even sure it's based on your conscious conception of reality. The question remains: does it matter? If your tools are faulty and your own self-awareness is debatable, then does it matter?

No…for success, it doesn't.

Successful people understand the hidden value of Brené Brown's statement. The one that started this chapter.

> *"Let go of who you think you're supposed to be; embrace who you are."*

So, even if their tools are faulty and they are aware of said fault, **THEY JUST DON'T GIVE A DAMN.**

Understanding What Self-Aware Means

When foolish visionaries and fortune tellers go on and on about self-awareness, they are mostly just channeling their inner gurus and, for the most part, it's a bunch of fluff. Why? Let me explain.

Self-awareness is defined as:

> *"An awareness of one's individuality."*

It's a concept that predates most modern theorists and is based on the neurological impression that we exist. Chemically, our senses perceive the environment; they, in turn, send an electronic signal to our brain and our neurons explode, translating that jolt into data that simply reads: *"You exist."*

Or, simply put: *"Cogito, ergo sum,"* which is Latin for René Descartes' big reveal...

"I think, THEREFORE I am."

Or, I perceive and I'm attentive to the world, I can sense it and I can interpret it; therefore, I am real. In a nutshell, the whole concept is based on the realization that you are real.

In biology or psychology, self-awareness can be defined as the ability of an animal to recognize themselves and conceive of themselves. The MSR (mirror self-recognition test), also called the red-spot technique, is a behavioral approach that was developed by psychologist Gordon Gallup Jr. in 1970 to determine whether an animal, any animal, is aware of itself.

What's the test and why does it matter?

The test is simple. An animal is anesthetized and then marked (either painted with a red dot or with a sticker) on an area of the body they normally can't see. Under the shin, or on the back, or above the shoulder. When the animal recuperates from that black-out (no doubt looking for who spiked their orange juice), they are given access to a mirror. If the animal touches or investigates the mark, it's an indication that it recognizes itself in the mirror and is aware of its existence.

If you've woken up, after a wild night *[insert your own Las Vegas experience here]*, gone to the bathroom mirror, and managed to identify that the reflection looking back at you is YOU, then you're self-aware. That's it. You deserve a treat.

So, when people say, "So-and-so is successful because they're self-aware," they either mean something completely different or they are simply equating prosperity to our innate ability as homo sapiens to identify ourselves in a piece of mirror.

What they mean is they are aware of their **SELF-CONCEPTS**.

In the next few sections, we're going to debate and investigate the idea of Self-Concepts and why it pivotal to our maturity, happiness, and success as individuals. We are also going to analyze the tricky thorn of Self-Image and why one clashes with the other.

Self-Concept

When people like Kobe Bryant, Steve Jobs, Oprah Winfrey, Obama, and all those paragons of triumph go on and on about their victories, they all share one common factor: they partly attribute their success to their understanding of who they are and, more importantly, what they embody.

We, as a society, due to countless and ad-nauseam ads and quotes, misinterpret the concept as their ability to be self-aware. We are wrong.

> *"Self-awareness in a person's psyche comes quite early. The moment a baby understands its needs and can voice them and comprehends that the world around them is creating physical pressure on their body is the very moment self-awareness starts to congeal. When a toddler understands that they have a body, that they can differentiate themselves from others, that's when self-awareness occurs."*
>
> B.F. Skinner, American Psychologist

What these paragons understood and then came to peace with is the idea of the SELF-CONCEPT.

A self-concept is a collection of beliefs about oneself. It is the foundation on which we create our identity. The more grounded in reality, the greater the fortitude of our palace. Self-concepts are those stones and bricks. It is a mismatch of definitions and practices, popularized by psychologist Carl Rogers and Abraham Maslow, that can be translated into one single unifying question:

"Who Am I?"

Our perception of ourselves as individuals is made up of thousands of self-concept principles. Of thousands of responses to that one governing question: "Who am I?" Principles and rules that we ourselves create. Guidelines that we hold true. This is our Constitution; our self-evident truth about ourselves. For example, I might say:

"I'm a highly creative and hardworking person."

I made a cognitive decision to assimilate that component into the recipe that is me. When someone like Kobe said, *"I'm a kick-ass player,"* he's making a conscious decision to not only to accept that about himself but to incorporate it into his perception of who he is. Our identity is partly composed of thousands upon thousands of realizations along these lines. Thousands of *"Who Am I?"* Some, as I explained before with that bizarre tale of VR nightmares, are faulty and have to do more with Self-Image; others align perfectly with our reality.

There are four key factors that determine each one of our self-concepts. Self-Schemas, Past-Self, Present-Self, Future/Possible-Selves.

Self-Schemas:

This is the raw data. The patterns or thoughts or behaviors we organize in our heads. It is how we interpret knowledge and create a framework for our comprehension of the world. For example, a schema can be defined as a social role or academic certainty. It might be what we learn in school and how that knowledge affects our concept of the world. It is how we feel like a part of society.

For example, if we are taught about the Bolshevik Revolution, and then read up on Karl Marx, we might identify with the likes of Che Guevara and end up putting a poster of him in our bedroom wall. In our teens, we might start shouting at the top of our lungs about the proletarian struggles and whatnots. On the other hand, we might read Marx and go, "Well, that's a load of...", and adhere to the idea of financial growth and capitalism. In both cases, we end up with a framework. We either became rampant Communists - identifying with their narrative and the feeling of being included within their party - or we become fervent Capitalists or Liberalists or whatever "ist" or "ism" you can think of.

And that goes for just about everything. We might identify more with Star Wars than Star Trek. With Marvel than DC. With Republicans than Democrats. There are thousands upon thousands of frameworks we weave into our lives. Each and every one cemented on emotions and education.

Self-Schemas are essential because they help us become members of society. We band under a collective narrative and this, in turn, drives us and helps us define how we view ourselves, how much value we place on ourselves, and how we wish we were or could be.

Past-Self:

It's how we perceive who we used to be. Not our collection of memories or experiences but us as individuals. How we processed emotions. Our level of maturity. Our tendencies and triggers. We don't look at the facts that made us - like the time our dad died and how it affected us - but the emotional outcome; how it made us feel. For the recipe, we don't go:

> *"Well, I'm a highly creative person because I have been pumping out content on a daily basis and enjoy producing marketing campaigns. I'm hardworking because I've been become accustomed to juggling multiple roles in my life since I was a kid and it has trained me to develop my work ethic."*

No, we simply say, *"I've become more creative and hardworking over time and I intuitively feel that."*

This temporal appraisal is faulty because we normally have negative perceptions of who we used to be.

We distance ourselves from a clear objective vision of who we were because we want our Future-Self to be better. That's why we normally fall into the trap of *"I'm better than I used to be."*

Present-Self:

This is how we see ourselves in the now. It's the emotions coursing through us right this very second. Are we content? Do we find fault in our existence? What can we improve?

The Present-Self is mainly constructed out of our emotions, our psychological triggers, and the madness that is swamping our existence at this very moment. It is one of the most insidious and tricky of factors. Why? Because, as a whole, our general perception of something, or a process, is based on a psychological fault in our way of understanding time… It's called Measurement and Error analysis.

As a whole, we grade an experience not by the entire experience but by the final peak of excitement. When we go out, and party all night, we mainly classify whether we had fun or not on the last BIG hurrah. If life were a rollercoaster, we would classify the ride as either good or bad solely on the final dip or loop.

Our Present-Self is programmed like this. It doesn't analyze the whole experience and myriad emotions that flowed through it; it just analyzes the end.

When we carefully look at our life, and our present, we have a preprogrammed bias to only accept and really study the emotions, feelings, and situations that defined this final peak. When analyzing the night, we don't take into account the great chat we had with our best friend and how that made us feel. We don't add into our formula the tasty pizza we had before we went out. We don't examine the moment when we came out of our house and stepped on dog caca. We don't include into our analysis the way our heart pumped when the waitress smiled at us.

We just arrive home, after nine hours out on the town, and analyze the night - at an emotional level - by how we feel at that moment. Yes, we might later do a tally of all the night's events, but it's that final moment that will really paint our Present-Self.

Future/Possible-Selves:

And finally, the most important factor: future possibilities. Why is this the most important? Because this includes our representation of who we might become, what we would like to become, and what we are afraid of becoming. This possibility is the drive of our existence…the ideal that functions as an incentive to change our behaviors and patterns.

So, what now?

So, we grab all those factors from the previous four points and create a map of ourselves. We draw our conclusions and make a framework of who we are. We write down a story of us.

"Ummm, my map looks funky... I doubt Obama's or the Rock's map looked like that..."

Here's where our self-fallacy or the lies that we tell to ourselves come in.

My question is the following... Where do you think we went wrong? Why are successful people better map-makers than us? Why are they more attuned to who they are and their different self-concepts? The answer is simple...

They don't cherry-pick their emotions. They don't try to paint their images into a narrative mold that makes them out to be heroes or makes them look good.

Self-Schemas, Past-Self, Present-Self, Future/Possible-Selves. They are well aware of every one of those key factors and what they mean overall. They don't add self-analysis and rewrite what happened and who they are. They don't back up and try to hide their shames or skeletons. They don't forget to include their woes or all the times the screwed up. They don't sidestep their Self-Schemas and what they've learned from life. They don't turn a blind eye to the immediate concerns of the Present-Self.

Successful people might be dreamers, spurred on by their future-selves, but they are fully aware of where they came from and where they are at right now. When Kobe's map comes out and it says, *"I'm a great basketball player,"* and it reads like the truth, it's because Kobe built that masterpiece on his training, his past experiences and hardships, his recognition of where he stood presently, and his will to reach a goal. He certainly didn't graph a map with just a pipe-dream in mind and nothing else.

Successful people are extremely conscious of the different concepts that make them who they are. They know their likes, dislikes, and who they are as individuals. They understand their tendencies, embrace their weaknesses, and always try to enhance their strengths. They use all these data points to craft every one of those key ingredients to create the rounded concept known as THEM. They then utilize all this information to customize their schedules and optimize their lives to obtain their goals.

A Better Map.

Did I lose you? Well, let's go back to your map – your analysis – of who you are.

You can't change your past, only reconcile with it and learn from it. You can't alter your future because it hasn't happened yet…but you can nonetheless tweak your present and hack your schemas.

You can utilize those two determinate elements to make a better you. You can hone your energies, develop your environment, Zen the hell out of your pet peeves, and adjust your different frameworks to push your present closer to your future-self.

Let's get practical. Grab a notebook. Not an IPad, not a cellphone screen, but an old-school notebook. The kind with paper and lines. O.G. writing material.
On the top of each page, you're going to write a series of questions. Mind you, you can go off-script and write as many as you want; this is just a small guide. Each question is designed to make you understand where you're at right now. To make you comprehend your present-self. I call this exercise, "The You Test".

THE "YOU" TEST

- **WHAT DRIVES YOU?** _____
- **WHAT EXCITES YOU?** _____
- **WHAT DOES AN AMAZING DAY MEAN TO YOU?** __
- **WHEN HAVE YOU FELT JOY?** _____
- **WHAT DRAINS YOU?** _____
- **IN WHAT ENVIRONMENTS DO YOU WORK BEST?** __
- **WHAT SITUATIONS DO YOU WORK BEST IN?** _____
- **WHAT COMES NATURALLY TO YOU?** _____
- **WHERE DO YOU GET YOUR BEST IDEAS?** _____
- **WHAT ARE YOUR PET PEEVES?** _____
- **WHAT TYPES OF MUSIC ENERGIZE YOU?** _____
- **WHAT INSPIRES YOU?** _____
- **WHAT TOPICS DO YOU LOVE TO LEARN ABOUT?** __
- **WHO INSPIRES YOU?** _____

And as I said before, the very limit of this exercise is the willingness to explore further. There really is no cap on the number of questions you can dedicate to this practice. More than a diary, this an Oracle of what makes you tick. Whatever interrogative tactic deepens your awareness is welcomed into your workbooks.

For the sake of transparency, I'm going to take my own questionnaire and jot down the answers right at the end of this chapter. Now, once you've realized that crucial first step, it's time to cut out the BS. There's a difference between reality and fantasy. A split between Self-Concept and Self-Image.

Self-Image is the mental image, generally resistant to change, that we have of ourselves. It is composed of the way we see ourselves, others see us, and how we think others see us. In most cases, this potential image is deceitful and has little to no concrete relationship to our actual reality.

For example, psychological illusions are mostly attributed to negative and poor self-image or even abnormal behavior.

> *"One of the most common phenomena that hampers psychological growth is the end-of-history illusion. The idea which an individual believes he has experienced the zenith of personal growth and changes in taste up until a precise moment, and that from there on his perception and individual maturity has stopped. Most people predict, regardless of age, that all fundamental changes in their personalities will occur between the ages of 20-30 years.*
>
> *People tend to see significant mental shifts in hindsight but fail to predict them; as such, a great deal is reluctant to change after a certain age on account of being satisfied with their current state.*

It's an illusion that's enforced not by our reality but by our perceived self-image."

Daniel Gilbert, Edgar Pierce Professor of Psychology at Harvard University.

In other words, we are constantly being harassed by thousands of faulty assumptions of who we are. We make flawed evaluations and imprecise measurements of the US and after a while, start to drag on our model of Self-Concept. This is the minefield we have to traverse in order to really unleash the potential power of this exercise.

Once we finish the notebook and our list, we need bullshit meters. Specifically, people who will objectively, through their knowledge of us and their intimate relationships with us, read through our list and call us on our ill-formed assumptions. Help us disentangle the illusions we have of ourselves from the reality that is us. In order of intimacy, from those who know us tangentially to those who know us in a more confidential manner: co-worker, friend, best friend, family member, spouse, or long-time couple. Pick those and run with it. Do this exercise at least once a year, while adding a bit of a narrative, to make this become your story. Track any differences that you notice over time.

Ish Under the Microscope

My full name is Ismael Verduzco III.

Or Ish, for short.

I was born into a humble Mexican-American family and learned the value of hard work at a very young age. Growing up, my family struggled financially, but they had just enough to get by. After understanding everything that my parents and grandparents sacrificed in order to provide a better life for me, I wanted to show them that their tribulations paid off in dividends through my achievements.

I am mostly driven by growth, progress, and impact.

I am extremely energized in situations where I have an opportunity to build something from the ground up and watch my work progress over time. Reflecting a bit on my life, I've been able to accomplish most when people doubted me, degraded me, or dismissed me. Since learning this, I've developed a way to spark this fire from within, without needing to rely on others for it.

I thrive in high-pressure situations where I'm against the clock and working towards a deadline. In a way, I work best when there's no safety net below me.

From Little League to college sports, I've always gravitated towards high-pressure roles like goalie, catcher, and anchor during my swimming days. I tried to play quarterback but ultimately I sucked at it, and opted for wide receiver instead. Still, a ton of pressure to make the catch and score.

This also brought me to be a part of student government, university executive boards, and president of multiple clubs and organizations.

In entertainment, I became a DJ. I absolutely loved the feeling. The pressure, energy and exhilaration.

In tech, this led me to work as the Global Social Media Lead for LinkedIn's two-billion-dollar business, Talent Solutions. Not bad for a kid from East LA.

Most recently, I worked at Snap Inc. (Snapchat's parent company), where I've been tasked with one of the tech industry's most difficult problems to solve: Diversity and Inclusion.

Simply put, if I'm not being pushed or tested, and I'm not growing as an individual, I get bored really easily. I hate boredom. I'm okay with rest and recovery, but I hate boredom.

Ish Under the Microscope, Part 2

Now, up until this point in my hair-raising analysis, there are a couple of things you might have noticed.

- First, I'm keeping my rhetoric, my phrasing, crisp and to the point. No literary BS, no flourishes, no embellishments; just straightforward assessment. What I have accomplished. Where I've failed. What drives me. What kills my mood. What I'm passionate about. Verbs, nouns, and almost no adjectives.

- Did you notice it? The fact that I'm talking in first person narrative? Using pronouns like I and me. The key to making a clear analysis is to frame your whole investigation in the first person. Impersonal, clinical, and deconstructive. As if you're being investigated by a homicide detective or a very astute psychologist. We're going to try to fix this in the following section. This helps our brain take a step back and switch from a subjective mindset to an objective one.

- Noun, followed by the verb. *"I did this;" "I felt this;" "I like this."* Active voice. I'm taking ownership of my actions. In passive voice, our brain instantly falls into the parameter of suggesting someone else or something else is the culprit of our woes and triumphs. We relegate culpability or ownership to an external force. The action is being done on us, or we are compelled to do said action. Active voice gifts us with the truth, we are the stewards of our actions, our past, our present, and above all, our future… We can't blame others. Here's a great way to understand if you're in active or passive voice: THE ZOMBIE DETECTOR. When a sentence has been written in passive voice, the subject is being acted upon rather than performing the action. The Zombie Detector is simple: if you can add the phrase "by zombies" at the end of your sentence, then you're in passive voice.

Here are some examples:

- The day was saved…BY ZOMBIES.
- Every Friday he gets paid…BY ZOMBIES.
- I was hired…By ZOMBIES.

- Finally, always, no matter what, encapsulate your points in past tense. You own the past, you live in the present; the future, meanwhile, is make-believe. Okay, now back to my self-analysis.

As we've learned above, I am extremely competitive. This can be both an advantage and disadvantage. In my teen years, this meant hours and hours of practice, sometimes on things that I wasn't even passionate about, but wanted to compete in at the highest level possible.

In recent years, I've become more aware of my competitive nature and now choose to use it sparingly; otherwise, I'd be like a scatterbrained squirrel, always joining unnecessary competitions that take me off course from achieving my goals. This is also why I no longer play video games or sports, nor do I dabble into areas that are outside my interest. If I'm challenged in something that I'm passionate about, then I'll hone in and study every aspect in order to put myself in the best position to be a top performer. This goes for work, career, business, hobbies, and many of my side hustles.

Most of my awareness comes from trauma and pain. Through the loss of my father and uncle during my early teen years, I learned to appreciate life and how crucial it is to make the most of every single minute that I'm on this planet.

Speaking of time, I don't like to waste it at all. I'm constantly studying myself, other high-performers, and people whom I respect for many different reasons. I believe that the better you're able to understand and take care of yourself, the more capable you will be at helping other people. Think about the last time you flew on a plane – the flight attendant always says to place your oxygen mask on yourself before helping those around you. Treat your life attributes as that oxygen mask and ensure that you've optimized them to foster a better version of yourself before you advise others.

A few elements that go into my ideal day include: learning of some sort, 7.5 hours of sleep, working out, and about 45 minutes of alone time to decompress. I schedule each of these elements into my daily routine, which allows me to be more present when I'm around others, more energized, and happier overall.

Above all, I am most drained by negativity and pessimism.

I'll try to avoid or drown these two out at all costs. This is why I refuse to watch the news on a regular basis. If there's worldly information that I need to know about, it will bubble up to my attention from my networks and I will go seek more knowledge about the subject.

Things that are both fun and come natural to me include promoting things that I believe in, building relationships, and truly understanding people and their patterns (one of the reasons why I minored in Sociology).

I get my best ideas when I'm in a public setting, yet unable to hear anything around me. Coffee shops + a badass pair of headphones bumping some house music while drinking a cup of coffee are perfect for this and where I spent most of my time writing this book.

I've learned that after a solid workout, it is really easy for to get into a flow state. Because of this, I switched my workouts to 5AM and use the morning momentum to kick off the first half of each workday. I have used (and continue to use) all of this information to achieve my goals.

2
GAME CHANGERS

"Goals are good for setting a direction, but systems are best for making progress."

James Clear

Neil Gaiman, critically acclaimed author and perhaps one of the most cherished English personalities of the last decade, once described his formula for success as such:

"You write. That's the hard bit that nobody sees. You write on the good days and you write on the lousy days. Like a shark, you have to keep moving forward or you die. Writing may or may not be your salvation; it might or might not be your destiny. But that doesn't matter. What matters right now are the words, one after another. Find the next word. Write it down. Repeat. Repeat. Repeat."

Hemingway concurred, back when he was slumming through Batista's Cuba, and rounded the whole sentiment far more concisely: *"You get up. You write 500 words, you celebrate with a daiquiri. Only cowards wait for inspiration."*

It's all about the routine, the practice, the rinse and repeat. It's all about creating your own hamster wheel and actually staying true to it. Practice makes perfect…but you first have to practice. That's the key.

Here's another huge revelation coming your way. Humans, in reality, are nothing more than a collection of biological, chemical, and neurological processes. It's that simple. And those very same processes are governed by a series of internal algorithms and recipes.

What Is An Algorithm?

In math and computer science, an algorithm is defined as a finite sequence of implemented instructions typically used to solve a problem or perform a task. They are unambiguous - that means they are fact based statements not susceptible to uncertainty, and are used to perfume calculations, data processing, automated reasoning, and millions of other tasks.
Let me give you an example, and bear with me because there's a reason I'm making such a big deal of this term:

Let's say you go to the ATM. You slip your bank card into the machine and punch in your pin number. A series of options pop up, and depending on what you press, you get a different result. You can withdraw cash. Make a deposit. Check your balance. Look at your last statement. Change your pin. Make a payment. Each option in and of itself sets up a series of digital cogs that will inevitably give you the result you went to the bank for in the first place. All of that is governed by algorithms. From the moment the ATM reads your card, links it to a database that needs your pin in order to grant access, all the way until you get a receipt for your operation, it's all controlled by algorithmic instruction.

Seems, simple, right? I'm basically telling you what you already know. The idea that all machines are governed by an exact series of mathematical recipes. But – and here's the thing – according to the life sciences, the algorithm for that previous transaction was set in motion way before you even reached the ATM.

> *"There's ample evidence that the brain may operate on an amazingly simple mathematical logic, one simple algorithm."*
>
> *Joe Tsien, Neuroscientist at the Medical College of Georgia at Augusta University*

According to the life sciences, the ATM transaction was set off by a series of deterministic or random algorithms in your brain. Those in turn sent a command to your appendages, which made you walk or drive to the nearest ATM. They then made you take out your card and slip it into the machine, and from that moment on, the biological computer (you) started to interact with the digital computer (the ATM).

Everything we do in life is governed by algorithms. For example, when we see someone we're attracted to, our reaction to that person is determined by an algorithm…one that has been mutating due to our environment, our heritage, our upbringing, and millions of years of evolution. We input into this algorithm certain data points and those in turn tell us how to react. Do we find that person attractive? Does something in them make us think they might be a potential long-time partner? Do we want to rip their clothes off? Do we want to take care of them in a nurturing manner? The way we react to them has to do with dozens upon dozens of factors. Factors that have to do with those nasty schemas we covered in Chapter 1. Factors that have to do with how we envision them in our future. And even factors that have to do with the way our cavemen ancestors evolved; vestigial remnants of our hunter/gatherer ways.

> *"Which woman could give him the healthiest children? This ensured that his tribe would multiple. Cavemen could size a woman up in an instant. Healthy shiny hair, sparkling eyes, good skin, good teeth, and ample bosom and shapely figure made for child-bearing. Women, meanwhile, needed a protector, an alpha in order to survive. These same attributes end up pressuring us in the long game of relationships. That's why some women fall for the bad boy and some guys fall for a ditzy blonde. It's something leftover from our ancestors."*
>
> Nancy Etcoff, PhD, author of *Survival of the Prettiest*

And our algorithm for such an operation is basically made up of dozen little blank spots where we have to insert these factors. Their smell. Their economical viability. Their body type. Their raspy voice. The way they remind us of someone. Their analogy to some social ideal.

There's a difference in how I will react, on an instinctual and automated basis, to, say, a silicon bombshell straight out of a Playboy centerfold - all curves, all lips, all sex appeal - to how I'll vibe with someone clearly as sexy but in another way; say, Natalie Portman, in an LBD[2].

But, no matter how you get off, it's still the same algorithm. A plus or an equal sign can't be altered…what you can do is change what you're adding up, yet the formula stays the same.

Why all the nonsense about algorithms? 'Cause that's the game changer. If we are all algorithms, and mutable at that, then why can't we simply change them? Why are we stuck with outdated recipes on how to interact with the world?

Habits, Rituals, and Routines

"Habits are the compound interest of self-improvement."

James Clear

Next, you will find some of my habits – positive, repetitive ones. It's important to be upfront about them before we start this section of the book.

We are all creatures of habit. The quicker you realize this, the quicker you're able to use that to your advantage. I've consciously built some great habits that are the foundation for much of my success. Some of these include working out – it's a mental reset that allows me to have so much more energy, clarity, and focus on everything else (relationships, work, side projects, writing this book, etc.).

---

[2] The ever fashionable Little Black Dress.

Another habit includes drinking water. I drink exactly 160 oz of water a day (I bought a 40-oz Hydroflask and fill it up 4x per day). Given that our bodies are mostly made of water, it's crucial to stay hydrated in order to function properly.

A habit that I've built over the past five years is actively learning on a daily basis through direct forms of media. The key word here is ACTIVELY. It's important to be intentional about the things that you care about; otherwise, they will be forgotten and deprioritized. My daily learning is made up of audiobooks, podcasts, YouTube interviews, Ted Talks, LinkedIn learning courses, blog articles, etc. I strive to learn every single day for at least 20 minutes; most days I'll usually squeeze in about two hours and, at most, finish a book from start to end. At the time of writing this book, I've been learning a ton through audiobooks published by people who have studied high performers and have worked with incredibly successful people. I've also been listening to interviews on a daily basis via podcasts and YouTube to learn how the world's most successful people have gotten to where they are during their lives.

I have a laundry list of others like my habit of sleeping 7.5-8.5 hours every night. This one was really difficult during the peak of my DJ career. Being out until 3 AM a few nights a week really messes with your sleep schedule and routines but I've been able to dial it back a bit in recent times.

I also listen to audiobooks or podcasts every time I drive except for Fridays and Saturdays. This habit has gotten so strong that it normally ends up being 100% of the time of my listening to content that feeds my brain when I drive (unless someone else is in the car and they're not down for that).

I'd be a bald-faced liar if I told you that you could alter your algorithms in such a way as to twist them on their heads and irrevocably change them. Why? Because, although these algorithms are partly based on those pillars of self-concept we built for ourselves (and why it was crucial to get that psychological exercise out of the way pronto in the first chapter), there are a dozen of other *nasty little things* that govern them. Things outside our purview.

What about bad habits?

I have a pretty bad habit of biting off more than I can chew. I think it stems from my desire to overachieve and, without having this turn into a therapy session, I honestly don't try to break the habit. Instead, I acknowledge its existence and dial it back when needed. Over-perform during my day job without working 100 hours a week. Knock my book out the park but ease up on DJ'ing for a few months to concentrate. It's all about work/life harmony, as Jeff Weiner, LinkedIn's CEO would say. How does work play into your life? There will be ebbs and flows at times, but knowing your tendencies is important so that you can make adjustments as needed. I love to excel at anything that I work on. It's one of my best traits but also one of my biggest downfalls because I become absorbed with my passion projects. At times, this means not working on something that I love for a little while so that I can reroute some time and energy into other priorities that are top of mind.

What nasty little things?

Glad you asked. I researched how Natural Selection and our Neanderthal forefathers screwed us over. How much did they screw us? Well, you know that need you have for chocolate? That insatiable need for sugar? Scientists have actually proven that our obsessions with sweets comes from an active genome that was switched on during our hunter-gatherer phase. Back in those bygone Flintstone days, fruits high in natural sugar were such a coveted commodity that whenever we had the chance, we'd cram one down our throat regardless of whether we needed it our not. When the monkeys allowed us to get close to the bananas, we made off like bandits and didn't stop chugging them until we were in a diabetic fit. That habit of thousand upon thousands of years changed our genetics…we tweaked our neurons to look at candy and go: *"EAT! Eat it before the monkey gets it!"* So, yes, you can use the tips I give you to curb your sweet tooth and get a handle on your dietary goals, but you will always have to deal with that evolutionary throwback. You will always have to deal with the baggage of our chimp forefathers. There's nothing we can do about that.

The same goes for dozens of other surpluses and extras left over from the time we were hunting wooly mammoths. You know that classic male-female argument of *"Will you just ask for help? We're clearly lost, Dan! What do you mean you know exactly where we are?"*

Well, thanks to the University of Utah, which studied various aboriginal tribes, the next time you get into a squabble about why you're such an ace navigator - even when you're clearly lost - you can turn to your honey bunny and say:

> *"Researchers studied the Namibian walking tribes…and guess what? Their forefather men scored better at spatial skills and navigation than their women. So, yes, I might be lost, but the reason I can't ask for help is because a part of me - from eons ago - still thinks on a genetic level that he's a walking GPS unit. Do you question Google? You can't blame me for how I was built… That's being a genephobe!"*

Yes, men have in their genes the need to puff out their chest and prolong a typical stereotype. Biologically, an errant DNA strand makes them think that they can find a lost continent by instinct alone. It's not their fault, it's just something that has been biologically ingrained into them; a vestigial strand of DNA. In a world mapped by GPS and clearly designed by infrastructure specialists, this ghost in the system is nothing short than a leftover bug from previous incarnations. It's like buying a Macbook and discovering it comes with a floppy drive[3].

As a person who works a full-time job in the Diversity and Inclusion space, I had to find another example that was a bit more inclusive of people, regardless of their gender association, so here's another one…

> *"It's a proven fact that primates began to associate alcohol to nutritional reward. The smell of fermentation led our brains to develop psycho-active rewards whenever we perceived it. These rewards translate to our pleasure sensors."*

So, yes, I'm having another beer… but it's not my fault, it's that of the first chimp that walked on the Serengeti in Africa.

There are hundred of little genetical landmines from those days that still have a role in our algorithm and the way we make decisions.

That's the first nasty hiccup. The second one has to do with our senses and the way we perceive reality. With how we become Self-Aware. We obtain self-

---

[3] Yes, super retro, I know. If you don't know what a floppy drive is, do a quick Google search and be amazed at how our parents stored information.

awareness partly when our senses kick in. When we can quantify and identify them. Sight, touch, smell, sound, and taste.

> *"Yeah, the five monkeys…or was it three?"*

First of all, it was three monkeys - the "see no evil, hear no evil, say no evil" primates - and second, you're not even in the ballpark. Since we were little, we've been taught that we interact with reality on the basis of five senses. The way we react is predetermined to these five senses. We communicate with someone through conversations and the way they see our non-verbal posturing. We vacate a room the second a foul odor hits us and we know someone passed gas. We go gonzo for a meatball sub because our tastebuds told us that it was just the right amount of spicy.

But, and here's the kicker…we've been deceived.

In reality there are at least 21 senses. At least. There's our sense of orientation - how some of us simply can't get lost in a new city. There's our sense of pressure and temperature. A sense called *proprioception*, which is, simply put, our sense of space. Our sense of equilibrium, our *equilibrioception*. Our vestibular system, meanwhile, has the ability to feel velocity – that's another sense right there. We sense the passage of time - *chronoception*. We sense electrical fields - electrocution. We compute dozens of senses every second and don't even know it. Our mind doing all the heavy lifting while we are oblivious to what it's really analyzing.

Right now, I'm writing this text on my computer and all my senses are activated. I'm interpreting what time it is. I'm feeling the pull of magnetic north. I'm hearing the people around me in this coffee shop. I'm trying to find the right balance of my rear in my chair. I'm tasting my saliva. I'm feeling the keyboard clack under my fingertips. I'm associating certain colors with certain emotions. I'm aware of all my limbs and can account for how my knees feel. I'm analyzing whether I should put on my hoodie - the A/C is kinda cold in here - or if I should move away from the air duct. There are dozens of senses, all unconsciously working inside of me right now. I'm not even aware of them. I'm just absorbing them and letting some part of my brain to deal with them.

And these senses have, like natural selection, a say in the way I interact and the way my algorithm functions. We can't alter these things because they are mostly outside of our control.

Habits

What we nonetheless can change are our habits and the way we learn and, more importantly, create meaningful experiences. We can alter our schemas - remember that word, it's going to pop up a lot. Every person that has been a success has a set of habits that they've consciously or unconsciously developed over time. Gaiman wrote on good days and bad days. Hemingway did his 500 words. Although artists, they didn't cling to the idea of inspiration. They didn't wait for some concept to plop out of the ether and tell them:

"This…write about this…"

They hunkered down and got to work. Sometimes they managed to climb into the moment. Sometimes it was a waste. Sometimes, out of 500 words, Hemingway only rescued six and sometimes, like Neil Gaiman once said:

"You re-read what you thought was rubbish and unearth a treasure."

What was their one pressing factor? What drove these two to win awards and become titans in their field? The idea of creating and nurturing a habit.

According to James Clear, the best-selling author of *Atomic Habits*:

"Habits are small decisions you make and actions you perform every day."

In a way, it is you adding a new algorithm to, well, you…or hacking a preexisting formula. A great example is learning a new instrument. Let's say you want to learn the guitar. Your algorithm for such an endeavor might state that:

A. You've never once picked up an instrument.
B. Your hands are small, so it might be a challenge.
C. You're tone deaf because your parents and grandparents didn't have a musical bone in their bodies.
D. You get easily distracted.

If you take each and every one of these into account, then there's a good chance that your algorithm states that you will suck at playing a guitar. Now, all of the above, all those annoying deterrents - a good guitar teacher will tell you - are conquerable. You just need to buy a guitar, start moving your fingers along the fretboard, listen to music with a bit more attention, and finally start to focus.

Sounds easy, right?

There's a reason why a recent poll stated that more than 80% of New Year's resolutions are abandoned by the second week of February...because they require you to actually work at them. Your climb to being the next Carlos Santana starts by practicing every day and forming a habit.

James Clear, and I'm going to be redundant here because it's way too easy given that last name, makes it *clear* that our life is nothing more than the sum of our habits. How in shape are we? How happy are we? How successful are we? How close to being Carlos Santana are we? It's all about our habits.

Habits co-direct and partly drive our algorithms. They won't change our genetic predisposition - in the guitar's case, that we can't tell a G chord from an A minor, or that our hands are tiny - but they give us a workaround for them. They can help us stretch our fingers and, after a while, identify one chord in the musical structure of a piece and put together its key.

Creating a Habit

In *Atomic Habits*, Clear outlines a road, or in his case a loop, for creating these ephemeral traditions and rituals. Four pillars on which he builds his surefire way of creating what he later deems:

THE HABIT LOOP

The idea is tied to the concept of feedback. If one habit leads to success, then success will inevitably double back on that habit and strengthen its foundations. If you start to play better, you will continue nurturing your practice habit because the pay-off is that you will play EVEN better.

Clear breaks down the Habit Loop into four stages. Cue, Craving, Response, Reward.

I've read countless books on the idea of habits, on how to hack them, and what makes Clear stand above the rest is the simplicity behind his method. It's an ideal, fantastic, and carefully orchestrated framework that even a sea monkey can perfect.

The Cue.

A cue is what triggers your brain. It's the signal that tells your brain that there is, at the end of the rainbow, a tasty reward. It is, if you look at the idea of self-concept, the fourth pillar...our future possibility. It is what we are striving to achieve.

This tiny bit of information jolts us forward. Why? Because it predicts a reward.

The idea of a "cue" comes from a psychological phenomenon called Pavlovian-Instrumental transfer. It is a classical learning condition that became famous with a groundbreaking experiment lead by Russian physiologist Ivan Pavlov. In 1904, Pavlov was awarded the Nobel Prize for the findings the experiment brought to light.

The idea was simple in hindsight but revolutionary back then. Ivan Pavlov grouped various dog species and hooked their gums to various sensors to quantify saliva outtake. Once every couple of hours, he would ring a bell and give the dogs a treat, something rewarding and mouth-watering. Each time this occurred, saliva flow would skyrocket.

What was Pavlov's discovery?

That after a couple of sessions, the treats were unnecessary. The animals reacted to the bell and started to salivate at the mere sound of it. He had conclusively conditioned the canines, on a physiological level, to the idea of a treat and then he had linked that very treat to a stimulus to which it normally wouldn't be linked. Pavlov proved that animals could condition their behavior just by envisioning a prize. They could change their physical makeup and the way they interact with their environment if they are propelled by that reward.

In psychology this reward is called a conditioned stimulus or "cue." It's not the prize itself, the object, but the idea you associate with it that gives it meaning and power.

In Pavlov's session, those dogs associated the sound of the bell to the tasty treat. In our case we might link one action or stimulus to that ideal we have of our future self.

The Craving.

The second step in the motivational chain or habit loop is the craving. Clear outlines the craving as the driving force behind every habit. It is a psychological urge for something that fate is holding back.

The only way we can actually form a habit is if we start to look forward to it. If we want to desire it eagerly. If it becomes something we lust for and covet above everything else.

Think about Arnold Schwarzenneger and his obsession with the gym during his peak bodybuilding days. Even fast-forward to present day – he remains a loyal gym goer and looks forward to it every day, while he is in his early 70s.

The craving, the desire, the ache for something, particularly for our dreams, has to be a force we simply can't shut off. A real and unaltered hunger that spurs us forward. If we can live without this pining, then its not a craving, it's just a "like."

The Response.

Let's talk about the third pillar of this little formula: the Response. Our good pal Clear defines the Response as the habit we are trying to implement or, better yet, adopt. It is the vehicle we will inevitably use to reach our objective.

It's the various actions you take in order to drive your vehicle from point A to point B. Over time, if you do that particular route over and over again, you begin to get better at it.

Why am I using that analogy, the analogy of the car? Mainly because it fits our parameters. First, we get this need to jump in our car, someone calls us, or a trigger catapults us into action. Our brain hooks that trigger up to a memory or a biological response...that's the cue. When our best friend calls us up on a Friday night and says:

> "Yo, Ish!! I just got us some tickets to see your favorite DJ perform at..."

Your brain doesn't go:

> "I'm going to see my best bud..."

Nope, it instantly churns up thoughts of the last time you two went out and had the time of your lives. It instantly makes a graph of that time, and measures it up to others and unearths an emotional response from you...which in turn becomes a chemical reaction. You're reacting biologically. You're mingling that memory with an emotion. You're that dog salivating when old man Pavlov fooled it into thinking it was lunchtime simply by ringing a bell. That biological response is the cue. It's what creates the necessity inside of you to go out there, despite the fact that your house is all warm and toasty, and brave the outdoors and the weather, just in case you relive that jolt of adrenaline or serotonin.

The Reward.

Now, after all of that, after that chain reaction, after your friend calls you up, your brain reminds you of that high you got the last time you met, and you're in your car driving through the night. You demand a reward...a payoff.

Something that's either better or at least up to par with the last time you went out with your best bud.

Rewards are the end results of all that turmoil. It's the reason why we're actually submitting ourselves to all the hardship. Every habit has a reward. You don't go to the gym because it's nice and you're having a grand time; you go to the gym because you expect that after a while you'll start to obtain the body that will inevitably lead to that future vision you have of yourself. You don't see hard work and sweat required to develop abs; you envision how the abs will look on your body and it keeps you going.

The cue is about noticing the reward, the fact that it exists.

The craving is about getting a tingly feeling in your nether regions for that reward. For wanting it like nothing else in the world.

The response is about what actions you're going to take in order to obtain said reward.

The reward is the magic that drives us forward. But, and here's the thing, a reward might also be a double-edged sword. Why? Because unless your prize is something simple, something you can obtain by going to the supermarket, then it requires sacrifice and patience...something some of us lack.

Warren Buffet once said:

> *"Each time I do something and score a win, I reward myself. It doesn't matter how small or insignificant that win was, I need to feel it as something tangible something I can look at or taste that will bring me pleasure."*

Why does Warren Buffet have this habit? Because it sidesteps a thorny issue in Clear's theorem...the fact that Rewards take time. Obtaining that golden ring takes time, struggle, and, above all, patience. So, meanwhile, you have to supplement that lack of payoff with a placeholder.

You go to the gym, you have a routine, but after months of trekking on the treadmill, you still haven't obtained your ideal weight. You're getting frustrated, you're thinking of quitting or maybe looking for an alternative, you're slimming down but you look at J-Lo and you're not even close. Well, unless you reward yourself, while you obtain the final prize, you will give up.

That's why, sometimes we need a battle plan. A battle plan built on stages and that rewards the struggles and actions of its troops after certain victory. Think of it as a war, one that can last as long as it needs to, with the final objective being to roll into Berlin and punch Hitler in the throat. You don't hold off on giving your troops a morale boost simply because Berlin is still a couple of countries away. No, you stage shows, you let 'em have fun, you buy them great liquor, let them have a night off, you incentivize them to go a little wild after each battle. Why? Because they'll fight even harder next time to obtain said tangible prizes... Hitler is a long way off, and peace is an ethereal notion, but an all-expense-paid pass in recently liberated Paris, with all the hotties, is something they can savor and touch.

The Neurological Feedback.

It's all about creating a loop that, like a perpetual motion machine, will inevitably change your life. It's about hacking you like a dog. After a while, Pavlov's pups had a biological reaction to the cue.

In 1996, a study by Harvard University determined that what really creates changes in our life aren't the rewards obtained from completing a goal but the adoption of a life-long habit associated with that goal...even if you've already obtained that reward.

The cue gets you running, the craving to reach the finish line fuels you, the habit of moving your legs spurs you on, the reward of the medal and getting there in good time pushes you onward. What Harvard discovered is that once you cross the finish line, you can take one of two directions. First, you can grab your medal and go back home, hang up your sneakers, and be absolutely content that you've obtained your reward. Move on to the next objective on your bucket list. The second option is that you look at your running time and go:

"I wonder if I can beat that the next time?"

This second option will once more fire up your pistons and push you towards a new marathon. That's how a habit is formed and that's how you actually make a life-long change.

A friend of British musician Mark Knopfler once told the press:

> "I'm that git from the Sultans of Swing song. While Mark was killing himself learning all the notes and scales. While he was working day in, day out with one objective after another, I was simply content with 'knowing all the chorus. Mind, it's strictly rhythm he doesn't want to make it cry or sing.' Mark made it habit, improving."

How to Build a Good Habit

The idea of making a habit is based on the acronym KISS.

> *"Keep It Simple, Stupid."*

The main reason why most people give up on their dreams is because the dreams are too large. They shot for the stars, with outlandish desires, but hardly stop to think on how to obtain that pie in the sky, let alone the fact that it's hard. New Year's resolutions come along and they go:

> *'This year I'm going to end December with a million bucks in my bank account."*

The idea of keeping it simple is getting the above statement and breaking it down into actual mini steps and then making them your objective. Maybe don't jump from 100 bucks in your savings account to the pipedream of becoming a multimillionaire. Instead, try:

"This year I'm going to make financially sound decisions. In January I'll take stock of my portfolio and see where I'm bleeding from...why my paycheck is always short. In February, I'll start to cut down on these leeches. In March, I'll use that very same money I was wasting on God knows what and make it grow... I'll open an investing account and give that dough to a banker that will do his level best to make it grow..."

And so forth. A normal person, for example, wastes over 25% of their paycheck on eating out, some even a whopping 50%. What do you get after all of that? What's your reward? A fast-food gut. After you spend at McDonalds or Starbucks, you're left with absolutely nothing. Let's say you start eating in or taking your coffee to work; suddenly you have a surplus of 25%. You have more money in your wallet. You can either save it or you can make it grow. In the second option, if the stock market plummets, well, you're left with the same thing Starbucks gifted you: NOTHING. But at least you tried and your finances are still the same as when you started the experiment.

But the takeaway is that you made simple goals you could shoot for.

Make your goal obvious. Make that image you're trying to obtain something discernible and accessible. That's your cue. Pavlov didn't train his dogs with an idea; he trained them with a delectable treat. Patton didn't promise his troops peace in their time; he promised them a bottle of Jack Daniels if they took the next village. And the dolt trying to make himself rich might fantasize with the million bucks, but he should first do his very best to obtain a bit of a leeway in his struggling finances.

How do I drive myself towards that goal? By making it attractive. That's how you end up craving something. The best way to crave something is to associate it with an emotional and primitive reaction; something that comes instinctually from your lizard brain[4]. If you want to want something, that something has to excite you. It is as simple as that. You have to unite the possible reward to your pleasure sensors. The troops marched on because they intermixed the taste of Jack with happiness and this in turn set off their pleasure sensors in their noggin. This is Procreation and Evolution 101. We procreate for multiple reasons, but there's a primary reason why the act needed to breed is so pleasurable, why sex is so satisfying and pleasing, because otherwise, as a species, we wouldn't have conquered the planet.

Make your habit easy. Make it something you can actually accomplish. Something you know is doable and possibly something you've already done multiple times. Why do people have such a hard time going to a gym and forming a routine out of that? Because most that start on that path have never once gone to the gym. They jump headlong into something that will inevitably bring about a great deal of struggle and pain and hardship. Now, what if they look back at the sort of person they are and uncover some physical activity they actually enjoy instead of going to the gym? Something that might come easy or even natural to them.

Make the end result satisfying. Make the reward something that actually produces pleasure, something that gifts you a sense of accomplishment and happiness.

---

[4] The Lizard Brain or triune brain is a model of the evolution of the vertebrate forebrain and behavior, proposed by the American physician and neuroscientist Paul D. MacLean. It's since become a bit updated, from a neurological point of view, but from a purely artistic perspective it sums up a lot of things. The Lizard Brain is basically that part of our psyche or our brain that's stuck on autopilot and driven by our most animalistic tendencies. The part that, for all intents and purposes, just wants to eat, have sex, destroy, and conquer.

Let's look at our would-be millionaire and view them under the KISS microscope.

Each of their objectives was obvious, something they can quantify and actually qualify at the end of each month.

- The **cue** for January, for example, is 'take stock of my finances.'
- The **craving** is extremely attractive: by the end of January they will have an idea on where they are wasting their money. Maybe they have some autopay options for services they no longer use. By the end of January, our friend will have a plan of attack on what fat to cut.
- The **response** is simple. As actions go, all they have to do is print out December's statement for each account and credit card they possess.
- The **reward** is extremely satisfying: the possibility of having a bit more dough in their bank account.

Suddenly, if the reward were satisfying, if our would-be banker suddenly found that they are saving 200 or 300 bucks a month just by cutting out the crap, they develop a feedback loop. Now, every month they'll print their statements and start to make conscious decisions on what to do with their cash.

Each month going forward, our friend will develop a better financial perspective. They might not end the year having grown their estate to a million bucks but they will feel satisfied with the end result. They'll feel assured and confident that the objective, which a year ago might have seemed a fancy, is now a possibility...so next year they'll double down and try again, only this time with a maturity they lacked the last time.

So, to recap, in order to make a feedback loop and create a habit, all four pillars of James Clear's methodology have to be simple.

Ask yourself the following questions:

- How can I make it *obvious*?
- How can I make it *attractive*?
- How can I make it *easy*?
- How can I make it *satisfying*?

How Do I Break a Bad Habit?

Ahhh, the elephant in the room. Sometimes the objective or mission isn't creating and fostering a good habit, but kicking a bad one in the butt. Things that are like albatrosses hanging on our necks. Millions of toxic little roadblocks we were either gifted with or we ourselves created.

This poisonous habit, to a degree, speak volumes of how we are and the type of person we see ourselves as. There's a reason why one phrase always pops up when we talk about bad habits...

"Bad habits feel so good."

Why is that?

Our brains are engineered to make us crave and consume. We are creatures that, on a crude level, work off an incredibly simple learning system called reward based. To put it succinctly, this system involves a trigger, followed by behavior and a reward. Sound familiar? It should if you've been reading this book.

These three primitive components show up every time we do anything, including a bad habit. Every time we reach for a cigarette or a cupcake, or check our Instagram feed when we're stressed. Each time we reach for one of those things, and in turn feel soothed or happy afterward, we reinforce the chain. Eventually it becomes automatic. This is how any habit is formed.

Now, here's the thing, the reason why we're hardwired to sink into bad habits. Why they perpetuate themselves over time and become so pernicious.

Our genome is a damn asshole.

It's as simple as that. Researchers at Yale, and others of their kind have discovered a trap that our brain has in store for us and the reason why we sink into bad habits. In order to battle with bad habits, we need self-control. We need a strong level of will to fight off the automatic reaction a cigarette sets off. Well, those Yale scientists discovered something amazing about the way our brain network is wired. The area of our brain associated with self-control, the prefrontal cortex, is the first to go "offline" when faced with certain key triggers...triggers such as stress, anger, depression, self-doubt, and so on.

In other words, the moment we need our will the most in order to fight off the calming release a carton of ice cream would bring is the very moment our brain decides to take a hike and go on vacation with that key element.

On a biological level, we can't count on our neurons to help us out. Yes, over time they'll come back into action but the critical part of that sentence is just that: over time. Meanwhile, until they decide to get their act together, we're left to fend off the wolves on our own.

We can practice techniques to manage these mentionable triggers. To get our stress levels under control. To tamper our anger. To medicate our anxieties and depressions. But the fact remains: we still have to deal with these bad habits.

We need to implement some sort of authority or oversight over them. Create a level of regulation to the point we can actually win a couple of battles over that damnable cupcake and malicious brownie.

Clear uses the opposite approach to his KISS mentality in crafting good habits for such a task. He doesn't gift us with the keys to analyze our internal conflicts; that's way out of his league. He does nonetheless give us a workaround in order to quash some of our bad habits...cheap and dirty tricks that really do work.

His idea to break bad habits is basically, to put it mildly:

MAKE IT A PAIN IN THE ASS.

Make it difficult, make it invisible, make it unattractive, make it unsatisfying. A total inversion of his previous method.

Rituals

Habits are automated actions, they come naturally and we don't really have any say in how they operate. Well, in most cases. Smoking is a habit; most addicts don't consciously know when they are lighting up a cigarette. Brushing your teeth is a habit; there's a level of operational action on your part - a little voice that tells you "pick up the toothbrush" - but in essence you simply accomplish the task on auto-pilot. We're not really aware of most habits. In many cases they are like poker tells, a quirk we organically show the world without any real requirement on our part. We don't doubt a habit. We don't acknowledge a habit. In most cases these constant massive actions occur without any input from us.

We snort, quint, chew with our mouths open, crack our fingers, go to the bathroom at a predetermined time, slip two teaspoons of sugar into our coffee, chew on the end of a pencil out of habit. Somewhere along the way we picked up this routine and now we don't even know we're performing it.

Rituals, on the other hand, are conscious decisions to act and create a routine. Rituals are essentially a sequence of activities involving gestures, words, actions, or objects. They are ruled by our empowerment of them, by our need to give them validation and form. By our desire to prescribe to them something sacred.

And there's a reason why we treat rituals as sacred – things that we value above everything else.

The word derives from the Latin *ritualis*, which means "that which pertains to a rite." It was a word heavily weighted with cosmological meaning. Rites were reserved for worship, sacraments, purification, oaths of allegiances, ceremonies, and coronations. They were steeped in tradition and, more importantly, gravitas. You had to sacrifice something in order to perform a rite and in doing so, you communed with something more important than yourself.

When the President is inaugurated and he vows to perform the service of his office, uphold the Constitution, and defend the American people, he's performing a ritual. He's forsaking part of his independence - becoming a servant of the people - and pledging his obedience to the founding fathers and the spirit of what it means to be an American.

When you perform a ritual, you're connecting with something greater than yourself; a religious being, your own intellect, the idea of friendship, the spirit of your nation, your inner ambition, your dreams.

Special occasions or holidays are governed by rituals - we call them traditions. During Thanksgiving, we base our whole affair not on the real-life events that led to the Pilgrims and Natives' peace, but on the misconceptions and narrative structures that give meaning to what it truly signifies to be an American.

When the British Monarchy invokes a "thousand-year-old tradition," it's just reviving rituals from the late nineteenth century. But, in calling on appeal of history - rather than the actual historical transition - it gives the ritual power.

Also, a ritual, unlike a habit, requires a conscious sacrifice. We sacrifice something to it. Our time, our attention, our independence, our happiness, our passions. This sacrifice gives it power.

It's in the sacrifice that a habit can become empowering and transform into a ritual.

Yuval Harari, futurist, advisor to Presidents, and award-winning autor, once gave a discourse on how he transformed a habit into a ritual and the payoffs he acquired from this tweak.

Harari had a HABIT of drinking green tea. Every morning he would start his day by brewing up a cup of green tea, dumping a couple of teaspoons of sugar into it, and reading the morning newspaper. He needed that jolt of antioxidants in order to get his blood pumping. He did this automatically, springing out of bed, putting on the kettle, grabbing a tea bag, and plunging it into boiling water. Then, he would absent-mindedly sip the concoction. One day, Harari started reading about the history of tea and suddenly came to realization that in spite of having been a tea guzzler all his life, he knew nothing of the stuff. The book spoke of spices and aromas and citric tangs…but all Harari could discern from his tea was the fact that it was incredibly sweet on account of the sugar.

So, he started taking the time to appreciate his daily habit. He started buying different types of teas and brewing them accordingly. He started to drink the tea sour and as is without any sugar. He started to sip the tea, without any distractions whatsoever. He wanted to comprehend the differences and really appreciate them. He realized that he was a fan of a particular tea whose seeds were fertilized by the dung of pandas.

Harari sacrificed his time, his focus, and his money, and made a ritual out of a habit. He transformed the idea of drinking tea from something that lifted him up and gave him a physical jolt every morning, to an action where he was emotionally invested.

A ritual is about creating an empowering habit and one you are invested in, not only physically but psychologically. It should be engaging, meaningful, and purpose driven. It most effectively connects you to your passions. It must inspire you, motivate you, and make you feel as if you're part of something greater.

Rituals of Successful People

Here's a quick list of the rituals some successful people value and practice:

- Measuring how much sleep they need in order to operate optimally
- Understanding how fitness plays a role in their lives and using it as a tool
- Aligning their passions with hobbies and working on them regularly
- Using meditation and yoga as to reset and remain grounded
- Being conscious of their diet and nutrition on a daily basis
- Building and fostering relationships over time
- Creating schedules in order to remain organized
- Finding out what form of relaxation works best for them
- Rising early in the morning and jumpstarting their day with fitness
- Investing in their development through courses, reading, podcasts, etc.
- Asking extremely thoughtful questions and actively listening

Questions to Ask Yourself

How do I build a ritual? What should my ritual be?
Ask yourself the following questions:

- ➤ What would I like to improve in my life?
- ➤ What goals do I want to achieve?
- ➤ What are my personal standards?
- ➤ How would I like to feel after each ritual?
- ➤ What empowers me?
- ➤ What am I willing to sacrifice?

Mozart wouldn't go to bed without having composed a song - it didn't matter if it was good or not. He would arrive at 11pm and sometimes wouldn't go to sleep until 5 in the morning. He sacrificed his sleep for his craft.

Voltaire would create cells, special places he could seal himself complete alone without food or water to concentrate. He would spend 18 to 20 hours in these cells.

Benjamin Franklin devoted each week of his life to learning something new. He devoted each week to a different virtue. Creating different weekly habits for different studies. One week he would learn the principles of cooking French food; the next he would devote himself to discovering all he could about diplomacy.

Thomas Mann set time for concentrated work. He knew that his most productive time was from 9am to noon so he would make it a ritual to get up early, have breakfast with his wife, do as much as possible, and then sequester himself in his study.

Hemingway was surprisingly rigid in his routines. He would get up at the crack of dawn, draft his stories longhand, and then, in the afternoon, he had a ritual…

Hemingway would type 500 perfectly publishable words and then have a celebratory drink (or two) at the local bar.

Agatha Christie's ritual consisted of renting out hotel rooms and burrowing inside until she finished a book.

Bill Gates watches educational films only when he's on the treadmill. "I need to sweat in order to really take them in."

Maya Angelou embraced the loneliness. She would live in a spartan room - "a tiny, mean room with just a bed, and sometimes, if I can find it, a face basin" - and write. She worked from 7am to 2pm. The only things she would take into the room with her were a Bible, a dictionary, a deck of cards, and a bottle of sherry.

Each one of them, and thousands more – including Charles "my ritual is to walk for hours at night" Dickens - sacrificed something for their craft. They sacrificed comfort. They sacrificed relationships. They sacrificed time. They were willing to bleed for their passion and create a ritual that would drive their dreams forward.

For them a ritual was something transcendent, something unique, something that emotionally linked them to their dreams.

Ish's Rituals

I like to string rituals together to build my very strict routines. Kinda like habit stacking, but I call it ritual stacking. Each ritual is a cue for the next one to begin.

Morning rituals: Wake up at 5 AM, stretch, pop my airpods in my ears and start playing an audiobook or podcast while I brush my teeth, then drink a glass of water, followed by 10 minutes of jump rope as a warm-up, working out for an hour while listening to an upbeat DJ mix — usually around 130 BPMs (beats per minute), then 20 minutes to decompress and do some thinking while my body cools down. Shower and get dressed, then drink my vitamins while making breakfast and listening to a podcast or audiobook and kick off the workday before 8 AM.

Evening rituals: Usually end the workday at about 5:15 PM, followed by 20 minutes of decompression, dinner with loved ones, work on a side hustle, then transition into my night time ritual. Brush teeth, wash face, Calm App, and my Philips Hue lights in my room shift the color to be a dark maroon color, which preps my eyes for sleep. Then I try to stop using my phone around 9:30 PM, lights out by 9:45 PM, and I'm typically out by 10 PM.

3
LEARNING SQUARE

"Know yourself and win every battle."

That quote from the top was ripped out of the first pages from the go-to manual for military strategy and power posturing techniques. A philosophical masterpiece that's still dragged out whenever someone wants to win an argument on how to proceed or sound like a cool James Bond villain. If you want to give off an air of elegance, feral intelligence, and sly attitude, then simply memorize a quote or two from Sun Tzu's *The Art of War*.

"Know yourself and win every battle." That annoying self-concept from Chapter 1 is coming back in the conversation. Sun Tzu had it down to a science. What did Sun Tzu and almost every successful person gleam? What other key factor did they believe, intuitively or not, was paramount to making a go at life?

EDUCATION or, for the lack of academia, LEARNING. Soaking up as much as possible, not only in your branch and discipline but from the world in general.

"Well, that's obvious."

You're probably saying. Well, you'd think, but if Jimmy Kimmel has taught us anything, it's that our level of ignorance, and our need to bask in it, has reached a zenith. You think I'm joking? Go to YouTube and check out how well we fare as a society when Kimmel sends his people out with a world map and a question: "Can you name a country?" Not one pointed to the US and over 50% were certain Africa was a sovereign nation.

What exactly does all of this have to do with the idea of bettering yourself? Well, it's simple – look back on what you've learned so far:

- How to properly assess yourself and create an in-depth analysis of who you are. Not just your good points, but all those hang-ups and foibles you drag along.
- Creating habits and exercises not just to achieve your objective but to improve who you are and quite possibly tweak all those emotional, psychological, or even physical things that seem like speed bumps on the road to life.

Now comes the hard part, the framework. The idea of embracing the first principle of discovery, the reason why we shrugged off the Dark Ages and embraced the era of Enlightenment...

"We know nothing."

Personally, I was decent when it came to school…and that's embellishing it. I didn't enjoy the prime reason one actually goes to school: the classes. I wasn't interested in most of the topics that I was required to study, but I loved the social aspect of it all. My parents and grandparents always stressed the importance of school and how it is a privilege - especially given that my grandma only made it to 2nd grade before having to start working. She often talked about how she wished she could have continued in academia. This nugget wedged itself in my mind, and I stuck it out and got good grades mostly to make my family happy. I would tell myself, well, I gotta at least get a 3.0 and, in exchange, I'm getting to participate in clubs, sports, and other fun activities.

I attended UC Merced and got my bachelor's in Management with a minor in Sociology. Again, in college, I wasn't super interested in a lot of my classes but did what I needed to do to get by - a ton of extra credit and office hours. I did love learning, but not in most of the subjects that I was required to take. Macroeconomics, Finance, Accounting, and so on. I was nonetheless drawn to Marketing. I loved it so much that I took a Marketing course twice. I'm not sure if going to college is for everyone, but I think it's **extremely** important for everyone to "learn how to learn" and what their learning style is. To understand, particularly in this chaotic world, how to shift and manage information. Nowadays it isn't about acquiring information and learning it, but how to value and interpret that information… There's too much out there and school should be devoted to training kids on how to make all this data, all these strands of info, fit into a coherent narrative. Learn what interests you the most and how you could potentially make a career or side hustle out of that. Learn what forms of media you absorb information best in. Develop a craving for knowledge in the subjects that trigger your excitement most.

Books, Books, and More Books

Oprah Winfrey, Bill Gates, Barack Obama, Deepak Chopra, Beyonce, Elon Musk, and basically anyone influential or successful one way or another, has a yearly ritual they adhere to: book recommendations.

Once a year, like clockwork, these titans will catapult into the limelight a carefully vetted list of books, novels, and papers they encourage their fans to explore. The world goes crazy when a guy like Gates reaches out to *Business Insider* and tells them:

> *"This year, I picked up a bit more fiction than usual. It wasn't a conscious decision, but I seemed to be drawn to stories that let me explore other worlds."*

And here's the kicker – one would expect the likes of Musk or Obama to single out a list of highbrow books. Tomes on Civil Rights, Evolution, Economy, and Future Endeavors. Well, they do, they gear out an amazing list of novels that could put a coffee addict to sleep. They also churn out, among the Pulitzer winners and Nobel Literary Laureates, a surprising amount of fiction and/or trashy novels.

Presidents and Heads of State, adding the Game of Thrones saga to their recommendations. Stephen King talking a mile a minute about Harry Potter. Taylor Swift admitting, *"Yes, I read 50 Shades of Grey...and the sequels."*

The important thing to them isn't just what you read, but the fact that you put an effort into the practice. The fact that you read, even the likes of the *Twilight* novels. Why? For two reasons:

1) There's always, like Martin Scorsese once said, *"something worth rescuing out of even the worst piece of art."*
2) Reading, above all other practices, heightens brain activity. Reading makes your brain work better and more efficiently.

Art, Education, and Brain Chemistry

And it's not just reading, but it includes every single human interaction as well – anything that grants you knowledge. Everything we perceive, one way or another, subconsciously or consciously, grants us an added tool. Even that Marvel picture you just saw might have gifted you with something that you may not have picked up on yet.

A study by Emory University determined that art not only heightens the connectivity in the temporal cortex, but it also increases activity in the central sulcus of the brain, or region responsible for the primary sensory-motor activity. Neurons in this area of the brain activate to create a sensation of not just watching, but experiencing the sensations we are witnessing.

But there's more.

Knowledge and its acquisition, through watching a film, reading a book, going to a concert, taking a new class, or simply picking the brain of someone we admire can alter brain tissue. In 2009, scientists Keller and Just uncovered that in focusing on learning something, anything, the brain creates more white matter; it rewrites connections and physically improves. We start to process information at a greater speed, with newfound intensity and even with augmented memory and a mutated attention span.

That's one of the multiple powers of learning.

"I don't care how good you think you are, or how great others think you are—you can improve, and you will. Being relentless means demanding more of yourself than anyone else could ever demand of you, knowing that every time you stop, you can still do more. You must do more. The minute your mind thinks, 'Done,' your instincts say, 'Next.'"

Tim S. Grover, author of
Relentless: From Good to Great to Unstoppable

The Tree of Knowledge: Hollywood Edition

Jennifer Aniston, the Hollywood star, "Rachel" from *Friends*, and one of the most successful female actresses of the past few decades, spends over $60,000 a year on acting classes. Despite the fact that she's won Emmys, Golden Globes, and Screen Actors' Guild Awards, has her own star in the Hollywood Walk of Fame, and basically knows everyone, *and* is one of the most sought after leading ladies of her generation, she still devotes a piece of her fortunes and time to her craft: to becoming a better actress and learning new tricks.

And it's not just Jennifer. Emma Watson not only finished her studies and completed a Bachelor of Arts, even after she hit it big with the *Harry Potter* franchise, but she went back to college at Brown and majored in Literature.

Natalie Portman enrolled in Harvard and has multiple degrees, including Psychology and Arts.

America Ferrera, BA in International Relationships.

And the list goes on and on and on. Dylan Sprouse, Cole Sprouse, Anna Paquin, Shakira, Claire Danes, Dakota Fanning, Julia Styles, Cindy Crawford, Oprah, Eva Longoria, Jodie Foster, and on and on and on.

And it's not just actors and actresses - although you go, girl, Mayim Bialik, with a PhD in Neuroscience from UCLA - but executives, CEO, futurists, acclaimed writers, musicians, and just about everyone who has ever been on the cover of *Time* and *People* magazines.

Why?

Because of the understanding that sometimes it's not just a question of what you learn but the fact that you're learning it.

Richard Branson once said:

> *"The reason I have so many fingers in so many different pies is that you can always take one finger out, taste and discover that something from that one goes great with that other one. The more you know of different fields, not just your own, the more you can think outside the box and make revolutionary changes."*

Compound Learning

Let's talk about building on interest and rewards, the idea of compound interest...but, as we've already gone the way of microeconomics with that great example from up above, the one about setting goals and doing the economic Macarena, we're going to skip left when we should have gone right and veer into gambling.

Why not go the usual route? Because I want to make this narrative stick, and let's be honest, bank talk is a dud.

You swing into Vegas, or Monte Carlo, or Atlantic City, decked to the nines in your most fly outfit. Just before hitting the casino floor, a leprechaun appears (don't ask why, it's called Magical Realism[5]). The leprechaun says:

"Well, ye bloody git. You found my pot of gold." You're fairly certain he's hammered because you weren't even looking for such a treasure. *"Anyway, me bucko, for that you know have the luck of the Irish. No matter what happens, you'll always get a better hand than the dealer."*

Then the leprechaun vanishes. Poof!

You go to the Blackjack table, put down a buck, and in a flash...

"21!" exclaims the dealer.

---

[5] Magical realism, magic realism, or marvelous realism is a style of fiction that paints a realistic view of the modern world while also adding magical elements.

Now you have two bucks. You let it ride. Second round, you get 11. He gets an Ace card up, and - following the house rules - pulls out a third card, a 10 of Spades, and flips his face-down card.

"26! Bust!"

Now, you have four dollars. The streak continues. Ten minutes later, your initial beat has gone from a single buck to over 300 smackers...a total of 299 dollars in winnings. All of it based not on your initial investment, but on betting with your subsequent wins, of letting everything ride.

Compound **[insert a noun]** works like that. Compound investment, compound car detail, compound earnings, compound therapy and...compound learning. You build up your repertoire, based on your initial investment. But the real gift of compound learning arrives when that leprechaun reappears.

"Oops, made a huge mistake. It wasn't you. The luck of the Irish was meant for someone else." He clicks his fingers and suddenly you feel every ounce of good luck slink away.

My question to you is:

"Do you cash in your chips?"

It depends. If you were playing on blind luck, not understanding the intricacies of the game, then grab your cash and begone. Now, if while winning, you started to pick up the rules, the tidbits, the rhythm, and the overall rhythm of Blackjack, by all means, stay. That's what you learned from all those wins. You learned when you bet and when not to bet. When to hit on a card and when to stay. When to double down. When to split. You learned, during that free-for-all where you had nothing to lose, how the game was played.

Learning is like that. You have nothing to lose. All you have to forfeit is your time. If you stay with it, if you apply yourself and start to understand the importance of it - what you're being given and how to harness it - then you won't need blind luck but just your own skills to succeed.

Let's break it down into a simple and bite-size definition that I came up with after all of my research:

> *Compound Learning is observing, picking up trends, asking questions, paying attention to nuances, implementing, and tying things back to whatever it is you are doing. It's learning in one job or interaction and implementing it in a future role, then taking those learnings and implementing, constantly iterating based on new findings. It's also this idea that tiny bits of learning can accumulate and compound on one another over time into tons of useful knowledge. All you have to do is put a little intent behind your daily interactions.*

Let's look at a great example: Kobe Bryant. When Kobe was 18 years old, he was still getting his basketball feet. He was wet behind the ears, figuring out his technique and fumbling at it. Back then, Michael Jordan was the superstar. Every ball bouncer wanted to be MJ. So Kobe goes up to his teammates and asks:

"What Makes MJ, Well, MJ?"

They give him a few pointers, and off to the court he goes. He practices his shots, his passes, his landings, etc. He competes and starts to see what works and what doesn't. What does Kobe do? Does he stop there? Nope. He starts, now with some newfound knowledge under his belt, to analyze MJ through recordings and videos. He mixes that with what he first discovered. He practices new shots, shelves old techniques, and goes through the whole thing once more. Each time he does this, like the basketball Jedi Knight in the making that he is, Kobe gets a bit better. He starts to understand the court, the dynamics of it, the velocity of the ball, and thousands upon thousands of other things. He scraps what works and then adds something new.

But here's the thing – Kobe doesn't just limit himself to practicing and getting a handle on the ball; he also starts to branch out. He wanted to be the best and, for that, he studied not only basketball and the sport he excelled at, but anything that might grant him the edge.

On April 18, 2017, Kobe Bryant wrote an article detailing one of the defining moments in his life:

> *"On November 12, 1996, Allen Iverson dropped 35 on the Knicks in a win at the Garden.*
>
> *On November 12, 1996, I played five minutes and finished with two points in a Lakers win at Houston.*

When I checked into my hotel room later that night and saw the 35 on SportsCenter, I lost it. I flipped the table, threw the chair, broke the TV. I thought I had been working hard."

Kobe then went on to detail the reasons why he was renowned as one of the hardest-working athletes in the world. A grueling exploit of learning from every imaginable source and then using those tidbits to up his game. To improve on it in every conceivable way possible.

He even studied the patterns of apex predators in the wild:

"I searched the world for musings to add to my AI mouse-cage. This led me to study how great white sharks hunt seals off the coast of South Africa."

Kobe titled that article, the one focusing on his Moby Dick obsession to beat Allen, "Obsession Is Natural."

He became a dog with a bone and thus became a multi-field athlete that learned all he could across various fields and cherry-picked what worked and what didn't.

Efficient Learning: A DIY Guide.

"What on earth would make someone a non-learner? Everyone is born with an intense drive to learn."

Carol S. Dweck, author of *Mindset: The New Psychology of Success*

Successful people intentionally seek out knowledge. They crave it at an ancestral level. Each piece of data they acquire is something new to process and digest. As such, they do everything within their power to hack their daily schedule to educate themselves on something new. They set aside time and energy for the sole purpose of learning, of getting knowledge streamed directly into their already massive brains.

Let's pretend that you didn't skip any chapter in this book. Let's pretend you read this book chronologically and didn't just zero in on the Table of Contents and jump straight into the juicy sections. If you've been following me so far, and allowing me to shove you into the madness I've derived from all my studies, then by now, you SHOULD have a good understanding of your habits, rituals, and routines.

By now you SHOULD have tweaked your daily life for it to be a more streamlined and efficient operation. Move a couple of things around so you have a more dynamic and productive schedule.

THE 25 MINUTE HACK

7:35 PM - 8:00 PM is great time to set aside for learning.

The average person in America spends **53 minutes** on **Instagram** in one day.*

25 MINUTES A DAY ▶ 5 DAYS A WEEK ▶ 125 MINUTES =

2.1 HOURS

The equivalent of a weekly college course.

LEARNING — 2.10 hours per week
COLLEGE CREDIT — 2.50 hours per week
INSTAGRAM — 4.41 hours per week

2.1 HRS x 4 WEEKS
625 MINUTES IN A MONTH
A WHOPPING
8.3 HOURS

x 12 MONTH A YEAR = 7500 MINUTES

125 HOURS

▶ For comparison, the average college course is about **35 - 40 hours.**

The key here is **consistency.** 25 minutes a day of fully concentrated learning, deliberate practice and inching forward is what will ultimately make a huge impact over time.

Put this strategy to the test with one of your goals for the year and notice how that dream seems a lot more attainable.

From SimilarWeb https://www.similarweb.com/corp/pro/

4
PUTTING IN THE WORK

Way back in the 1970s, Anders Ericsson cooked up the mother of all boring experiments. Ericsson was making a name for himself. He was on a high, coming off some interesting experiments and cooking up new ones. The psychologist was born in Sweden in 1947 and became enamored as a small boy of the mechanics behind the human psyche. This love became a lifelong passion. A passion that lead Ericsson into the field of psychology. He worked his ass off and, after numerous publications and accolades, he started to gain some notoriety. So much so that he became a Conradi Eminent Scholar, which is a huge deal. But the point is, he began to write his own ticket.

So, with this freedom, this newfound clout to do anything in the world, Ericsson took an unexpected turn. He devised the most boring and innate experiment in the world.
Ericsson went and gathered a kid called Steve Faloon.

"Steve," he said. "This is really, really, really simple. No! We're not going to talk about your mom! Do you think that's the only thing psychologists do?

Well, yes, but most of the times it's just to mess with you. Anyway, Steve, the experiment is incredibly simple. All you have to do is memorize random strings of numbers. That's it."

Ericsson's only interest was to document how many numbers Steve could keep in his head through consistent practice.

Now, I know what you're thinking...that's it? That's the breakthrough experiment that you decided to include in this book?

Patience, grasshopper, there's a rhyme to all of this. You see, back then, common wisdom dictated that a regular person could only hold seven or eight random bits of information in their head at any given time. This same research is one of the key facts that sprung telephone companies to limit phone numbers to eight digits. This pivotal fact had been proven time and time again.

Anyway, if anything, Steve was giving credence to the whole idea. The kid could reliably recite back strings of seven to eight digits. At nine, his head would get all jumbled up and he would start to struggle. By 10, Steve couldn't remember a thing.

Every day, Ericsson would sit with Steve and read him random and chaotic strings of numbers at a rate of one per second, and Steve would in turn remember and recite them back to him. And always, after eight, he would start to falter.

Four sessions in, each more than an hour, and Steve was no better than on day one.

Then came the fifth session. Here it all changed. Ericsson made the breakthrough that would cement him as an authority in a specialized field he would later spearhead.

Suddenly, Steve succeeded at recalling his first 10-digit string. Flabbergasted and stunned, Ericsson paused the experiment let Steve unwind and recited a whole new random chain of digits. It had probably been a fluke. This time, Steve, even to his own amazement, didn't bat an eye and actually managed to beat his previous record by one. Now Steve could remember 11 numbers.

'Big whoop,' you're probably thinking, 'so Steve is slowly becoming Rain Man.'

Think about it, it's not a trivial thing. Up until that point, the big shots had determined that the cut-off for our memory was seven, maybe eight. We could only remember that many numbers. Then, boom, Steve is suddenly slinging out digits like he's counting cards. He went from 7 to 11...that's 57% over the average, and over what he could accomplish. Steve had improved in that field, against all of science and modern thinking, by 57%.

By his 200th session with Ericsson, Steve could recite, without making a mistake, strings of up to 82 random numbers.
Steve didn't have any special gifts or mutant powers. He wasn't a mathematician. He was a regular Joe. Ericsson went and repeated the experiment with other subjects and his findings were constantly proven.
Ericsson called this technique "Deliberate Practice." He devoted his career to studying experts in the fields of arts, music, sports, medicine, chess, and just about any area in which people had a talent some would call "magical."
He focused exclusively on extended deliberate practice and, more to the point, what he coined as "high concentration practice beyond one's comfort zone."

He went and made a field out of his less than trivial experiment. With Bill Chase, he developed the "Theory of Skilled Memory." With Walter Kintsch, he extended this theory into the phenomenon of long-term memory.

He published dozens of papers on the subject and quite a few books, among them *The Cambridge Handbook of Expertise and Expert Performance*.

Oh, and Steve? He kept working and actually managed to improve his memory and remember over 100 random numbers.

> *"People believe that because expert performance is qualitatively different from a normal performance, the expert performer must be endowed with characteristics qualitatively different from those of normal adults. ... We agree that expert performance is qualitatively different from normal performance and even that expert performers have characteristics and abilities that are qualitatively different from or at least outside the range of those of normal adults. However, we deny that these differences are immutable, that is, due to innate talent. Only a few exceptions, most notably height, are genetically prescribed. Instead, we argue that the differences between expert performers and normal adults reflect a life-long period of deliberate effort to improve performance in a specific domain."*

Practice makes perfect...if done right.

One of Ericsson's core findings was that it is not repetition that makes a person an expert but how that person practices.

In other words, if you want to develop a skill, and improve at said skill, it really doesn't matter if you keep hammering at something time and time again, but *how* you do the hammering.

An expert, Ericsson uncovered, breaks down the skills that are required to be a god in his field and focuses on improving those talents in chunks during practice or day-to-day activities. They often pair this with immediate coaching feedback. Another important feature of deliberate practice lies in continually challenging yourself by mastering expressions of that skill that are outside your league or simply too hard.

> *"Grit. It's about grit. It's about a student focusing with will and determination on material which they struggle with. Grit allows a student to persevere and succeed in the face of adversity."*

Angela Duckworth, Author of *Grit: The Power of Passion and Perseverance*

Talent is overrated.

The real gift of Ericsson's studies is that it definitely proves that talent, innate, inbred talent, the sort that comes with your meal ticket attached to it, comes up short if faced with Deliberate Practice.

Why? Mainly because cognitive thinking and behavioral theories, the basis for Deliberate Talent, demand that in order for you to improve in your desire skill, you're no good to begin with. Simple.

In cognitive theory, excellent performance results from practicing complex tasks that produce errors. Trial by error is a pivotal piece to learning something new.

Such errors provide the learner with rich feedback that results in scaffolding for future performance. This reality ultimately explains how a learner can become an expert.

Another important facet, one that gives you and edge over talent, lies in a trap native to talent.

Maintenance is an important facet of Deliberate Practice. Skills fade with non-use. They fizzle out. This phenomenon is often referred to as "being out of practice." It is a common problem that assails people with natural talent.

The Genetical Breaking Point

One of the benchmarks of Deliberate Practice, and a big myth some folks are peddling is the idea that all you need in life to succeed are hard work and grit.

What most people and self-help wizards like to sell you is the idea that there is no limit to what you can accomplish with Deliberate Practice. Sadly, that's a bald-faced lie.

Deliberate Practice doesn't mean that you can fashion yourself into anything; it just means that with enough work, dedication, and effort, you can develop your skills in a remarkable way. There's still a glass ceiling called genetics. Your genes ultimately cap the amount of progress you can develop in a field. They are your limits.
You can't go against biology…well, you can, a bit, but not much. You have to work with what you have. Know yourself and all that.

"However, while genetics influence performance, they do not determine performance. Do not confuse destiny with opportunity. Genes provide opportunity. They do not determine our destiny. It's similar to a game of cards. You have a better opportunity if you are dealt a better hand, but you also need to play the hand well to win."

James Clear

"You Should Be Gettin' It…"

If you're not a "Too Short" fan, then you missed the reference, but it's appropriate. Why? Because in order to understand how long it takes an average person to transform into an all-star, we need to talk about music.

John Hayes, a renowned cognitive psychology professor at Carnegie Mellon University and another of Ericsson's peers, wanted to clear that question up. The mystery of how long it would take an individual to switch from being an amateur into a master. From apprentice to Jedi.

Hayes started to examine successful composers throughout history for the answer. Folks like Bach, Mozart, Beethoven, and dozens more. He created a framework based on multiple factors to analyze these personages and perhaps gleam the truth he was after.

Hayes gathered 500 famous musical pieces, the ones that were frequently played by symphonies around the world and considered masterpieces in the field. Then, he filtered these pieces by composer. The 500 masterworks were in fact written by 76 composers. These 76 creators became the basis of Hayes' studies.

Hayes studied the musical cabal's timeline, mapping out their career. He was after the exact numbers of years it took each composer to finally have a HIT.

What Hayes discovered was that, with three exceptions, most of these titans produced their first masterpiece after 10 years of venturing into music. And the exceptions? They crafted their pieces after nine years of effort. Not a single one of them created any significant work without first putting in a decade or so of practice. We're talking about people like Wagner, Mozart, Beethoven.

Hayes then used the same parameters and transported the study into the field of painting and famous painters. He came back with the same results. Hayes, stumbling onto something significant, then went after poets and writers. The results? The same.
Hayes called this period of growth, hard work, and little recognition, as the "ten years of silence."

A couple of papers afterwards, Ericsson confirmed Hayes' findings.

> *"You need to put in 10,000 hours of work to become an expert in your field."*

Time Is On Your Side

Here's a rock reference this time, courtesy of the Rolling Stones.

So, 10 freaking years. That's what you need in order to become the best in your field. You're probably blowing a raspberry and saying:

"Kendrick Lamar, Taylor Swift, J. Cole, Beyonce, DJ AM, Bad Bunny, Maná. They didn't need 10 years."

Well, they sort of did. Plus, some of their hits are collaborative efforts. Beyonce needed a staff of 18 to produce and write "Single Ladies (Put a Ring on It)." Queen, with four members, only needed 15 years' mastery of their trades to churn out the pantheon of musical pieces: "Bohemian Rhapsody."

But there is hope. As Hayes, Ericsson, and other researchers started to do follow-ups and dug deeper, they came upon a couple of factors that flew against their results. Well, not so much factors but personalities. They discovered that success, primarily in this day and age, isn't chained to just time. There are other key characteristics that are paramount to achieving what Queen did in less time.

These characteristics are fairly new and throw the researchers' findings out the door.

To understand what these factors were, and how to maximize your potential, we have to look at the training habits of NBA superstar Kobe Bryant.

Kobe won two Olympic Gold Medals, five NBA Championships, and amassed a net worth of over $200 million during his career. If it hadn't been for a tragic airplane accident, there's no doubt in many of his friends, teammates, and adversaries that Kobe would have kept breaking records and redefining the sport.

In 2012, Kobe went to the Olympics as a selected member of Team USA. During this pivotal time in his career, Kobe and the rest of the team were being trained by a plethora of professionals, amongst them a man named Robert.

A couple of year ago, Robert posted on Reddit his impressions of Kobe and what it ultimately took him to achieve his god-like status on the court.

"I was invited to Las Vegas to help Team USA with their conditioning before they headed off to London. I've had the opportunity to work with Carmelo Anthony and Dwayne Wade in the past, but this would be my first interaction with Kobe.
The night before the first scrimmage, I had just watched "Casablanca" for the first time and it was about 3:30 AM.

A few minutes later, I was in bed, slowly fading away, when I heard my cell ring. It was Kobe. I nervously picked up.

"Hey, uhh, Rob, I hope I'm not disturbing anything right?"
"Uhh, no. What's up, Kob?"
"Just wondering if you could help me out with some conditioning work, that's all."
I checked my clock. 4:15 AM.

"Yeah sure, I'll see you in the facility in a bit."

It took me about twenty minutes to grab my gear and get out of the hotel. When I arrived and opened the room to the main practice floor, I saw Kobe. Alone. He was drenched in sweat as if he had just taken a swim. It wasn't even 5:00 AM.

We did some conditioning work for the next hour and fifteen minutes. Then we entered the weight room, where he would do a multitude of strength training exercises for the next 45 minutes. After that, we parted ways. He went back to the practice floor to shoot. I went back to the hotel and crashed. Wow.

I was expected to be at the floor again at about 11:00 AM.

I woke up feeling sleepy, drowsy, and pretty much every side effect of sleep deprivation. (Thanks, Kobe.) I had a bagel and headed to the practice facility.

This next part I remember very vividly. All of the Team USA players were there. LeBron was talking to Carmelo, and Coach Krzyzewski was trying to explain something to Kevin Durant. On the right side of the practice facility, Kobe was by himself shooting jumpers.

I went over to him, patted him on the back, and said, "Good work this morning."
"Huh?"
"Like, the conditioning. Good work."
"Oh. Yeah, thanks, Rob. I really appreciate it."
"So when did you finish?"
"Finish what?"
"Getting your shots up. What time did you leave the facility?"
"Oh, just now. I wanted 800 makes. So yeah, just now."

And after all of that, after not sleeping a wink, Team USA had practice.
So, what did you learn from all of that? Aside from the fact that Kobe probably had Red Bull for blood.

KOBE BRYANT: HOW TO BE THE BEST

800 Kobe had a daily goal: 800 made jump shots.

1 Expert trainer giving him feedback.

2 WORKING ON THE

10,000 HOURS PRINCIPLE or Ten Years Motto on overdrive.

3 Using **Biofeedback** (smartphones and watches); video equipment; state of the art sportswear.

4 Developing other skills and muscles groups, not just focusing on shooting hoops.

YOGA　SPRINTING　STRENGTH TRAINING　MEDITATION　MARATHON RUNNING　PILATES　CYCLING

5 Working **outside his comfort zone.** (In different gyms, stadiums, even in saunas).

Your Comfort Zone

Where the magic happens!

6 **Mentorship:** Jordan, Russell, Kareem, Musk, and even the King Of Pop.
Jackson on the phone with Kobe: "keep doing what you're doing. Don't be normal... don't dumb it down."

7 In order to hear the subtle bounce of the ball on the court and react to its bounce by distance and vectors, **Kobe trained his ears.** He became so adept at it that he ended up teaching himself **how to play piano pieces.**

"'Casablanca' is a great movie."

Yes, sure, that too... but you missed the point. Let's take a look at that talent critically. Let's analyze what exactly Kobe was instinctually doing and how it fit organically into Ericsson's ideals of Deliberate Practice.

- ✓ Kobe had a goal: 800 made jump shots.
- ✓ He had an expert trainer giving him feedback.
- ✓ He was working on the 10,000 hours principle or ten years motto, only in high speed.
- ✓ He was developing other skills and muscles groups, not just focusing on shooting hoops.
- ✓ He was working outside his comfort zone.

And, although not set but implied, Kobe was working out in the 21st century.

21st Century Dynamics

Why is this last bit of info important? That scrap of info was relegated as an afterthought, so much so that Robert didn't even mention it, we had to intuit it. Why is the fact that Kobe, as with so many other artists, athletes and experts, is a product of the 21st century so important?

Let's go back to Hayes' study and see if you spotted the one thing he might have done wrong...did you find it? Nope?

Well, the main source of argument and critical contention to Hayes' findings has to do with the time period used to filter his text subjects from: the late 17th to the early 19th century.

And, like Tupac once said - and artist Hayes didn't map - *"We gotta start makin' changes."*

Kobe, Beyonce, Swift and all that lot have technology on their side. They have expert scientific help in their corner. They have the resources of industries clearly crafted to make them better.

When Taylor Swift practices her vocals and songwriting skills, she does it with the backing of not only the best individuals in her sphere but the best technology that she can afford...tech wonders that in most cases are at the public's fingertips.

Let's go back to Kobe, as he's our lighting rod right now. When Kobe was jumping on that court, he had cushioned sneakers, clothes that had been hacked by Nike, isotonic sports drinks, and a smartphone brimming with apps to help improve...not to mention the internet as his wingman in case he needed to look something up. Kobe had been worked over by a team of nutritionists with the latest inside scoop on what makes an athlete's ticker tick to 110. Kobe had gadgets that calculated his blood rate and oxygen levels, and even filmed himself so he could critically examine his faults.

Kobe, like Swift, and almost everyone else were products of their times. When Beethoven's hearing started to deteriorate, he took it like a champ, and understood that his days as an artist was basically over. When Bono's voice box was shot, way back in the late 90s, he went to a series of specialists and came out two years later with one of U2's finest albums: *All That You Leave Behind*. A physical setback, something that would have ended your career less than a century ago, is just that, a "setback." Nowadays, old Ludwig would have had a small surgical sound piece grafted onto the back of his ear. This mic, through bone conduction, would have restored most of his hearing. With a few upgrades, even this receptor would have improved Beethoven's hearing to the point that it might have been better than the one he was born with.

We are no longer constrained in deliberate practice by the same factors as our forefathers. Now, we have technology, which is moving at a rapid pace, on our side. As I write this, AI tech has improved to such a degree that there are study apps that learn about you while you're using them. They start to modify their curriculum to better suit your particular temper. They tell you what time of the day you're most likely to soak up knowledge and practice better, they adapt their speech patterns to your personality, and they create challenges that are tailor made for your unique sensitivities.

And, as technology advances, everything starts to link up. Your smartwatch will know more about you than you do about yourself, and it will assist you in a unique and personalized way through your deliberate practice periods.

That is the reason why Kobe and his contemporaries aren't restricted by the 10-year rule...and neither are you.

Still not sold? Well, this book is a clear example of how much we have advanced from those dark days. Back in Mozart's time – hell, back in Elvis' time – there was little research done on the subject of learning. Now, you have psychologists, neurologists and cognitive scientists dissecting the whole phenomenon and discovering this about the process we didn't even know existed.

This book is a testament of how much we have evolved and why the 10-year rule, although valuable, can be circumvented.

Putting It All Together

"I never viewed myself as particularly talented. Where I excel is ridiculous, sickening, work ethic. You know, while the other guy's sleeping, I'm working."

Will Smith, American actor

The truth of the matter, when you get down to it, is that you can work at something until your fingers bleed, your eyeballs fall out of your head, and you get a nasty feeling in the pit of your stomach because basically, you're sick and tired of practicing like crazy. Here's the thing, you might work your fingers down to the bone but unless you're practicing intelligently, you're just wasting your time.

Frida Kahlo suffered from polio during her childhood - some sources even claimed that she had to deal with spina bifida, which caused dysmetria in her right leg. As a teen, Frida's whole medical drama was aggravated after a particularly nasty road accident. She spent all her life in bed and in severe pain. Her pain, she constantly said, inspired the beauty and majesty of her work. She fashioned her hardship into a fire. It took her time, it took her adapting to her body - even when it was betraying her - and, above all, it took her putting it all together.

"My painting carries with it the message of pain."

Andrea Bocelli has sold more than 75 million records. He was born with congenital glaucoma, or partly blind. At age 12, a blow in a football game left him completely blind. He adapted to his new life and devoted his life to poesy and artistry. He focused on channeling his anger and sadness towards mastering his other senses…particularly his sense of sound. Bocelli, aside from those 75 million records, managed to study law, devote his life to music, and become one of the most influential tenors of his time. Hell, he even has a beach named after him in the Adriatic.

> *"Destiny has a lot to do with it, but so do you. You have to persevere, you have to insist."*
>
> Andrea Bocelli

Steve Nash, Michael J. Fox, Alex Zanardi, Aaron Fotheringham, Beethoven, Nick Vujicic, Stevie Wonder, Ray Charles, FDR, John Hockenberry, Marlee Matlin, Helen Keller, Sudhan Chandran. Each and everyone of them was born with a huge disability and made a killing. They became legends. They put in the time, adapted to their circumstances and, to put it mildly, flipped fate and destiny off.

But, what about a minor, almost inconsequential, disability? What about when we're not discussing the trials of learning to live without any legs or adapting to being blind? Most of us have one startling fact in our biology we simply cannot change, something passed on by our fathers or mothers that's not a handicap but a huge pain the rear…something innocuous but ultimately sets us back. Maybe we have a wild chromosome that makes us favor our gut and drives us towards obesity. Maybe we have an errant DNA strand that makes it hard for us to develop muscles. Maybe we're simply endowed with a high IQ. Maybe our pigmentation makes us susceptible to UV rays. So many maybes outside our scope of control.

What happens when that tiny genetical hiccup throws a monkey wrench in our dreams and plans? What happens when we want to become a marathon runner but our sweat glands betray us and we dehydrate at a faster pace than the average Joe? It's not a Kahlo handicap, but it's still something pernicious that affects us directly. What then?

Let's talk about John Mayer's monstrous hands.

The Mayer Dynamic

Eric Clapton once called John Mayer "one of the greatest guitar players in the world." And, although it might pain you to admit it, knowing the somewhat smartypants attitude of Mayer - and the fact that he sometimes might rub people the wrong way - there's no real denying the fact that the fella' can jam.

Mayer has created his own guitar technique, defying a slight physical setback and a few roadblocks, and adapting an instrument to his own peculiar way of playing. Unlike other players, Mayer created his own technique and didn't mold himself into the standard way of playing acoustic guitar. That's why he is considered a musical genius…and why folks like Billy Joel, Eric Clapton, Billy Gibbons, and dozens of other fret-shredders dip their hats in the presence of that punk.

One of Mayer's most intriguing numbers is "NEON" – a nemesis to almost all guitar players. It's a fingerpicking masterpiece where Mayer dances through the strings, maintains an eclectic beat, uses jazz chords, does a peculiar pulse - one that he invented that uses the guitar as a percussion instrument - and he pulls all of this up while singing melodically.

And this is just one of Mayer's classic tunes.

Now, why is this important to this chapter? Because, as musicians are prone to point out, Mayer is an anomaly. He stands out from the pack. The way he plays the instrument is all over the place and really goes against the norm.

A quick example is the way he fingerpicks. That when a guitarist forgoes the pick and uses his fingers to pull at individual strings; tapping pulses while also plucking melodies in the lower strings. It's something hard, and something that in most musical schools is taught this way: the thumb is used for the lower pitch strings (the top three), while the pointer, ring, and middle are used for the higher pitches/lower strings. Finally, the pinky is employed as an anchor against the wooden frame of the guitar. Mayer meanwhile skips this train of logic, and only uses two fingers - the thumb and middle. He does millions of little things with these two fingers. He basically plays more experienced players that employ all their little pigs under the table with just two digits.

But why?

When Mayer was in college, studying music and trying to rock out, his teachers basically labeled him as "incredibly talented but with a problem that sets him back."

Mayer has huge hands, which for an instrument like a guitar can be a bit bothersome. Fingers start to get in the way of other fingers, the instrument feels cumbersome, the neck doesn't slide properly, and when you try to make a chord, flesh rides on flesh and numbs the strings. In other words, Mayer, although talented, had to deal with a genetic hiccup.

What did Mayer do?

Well, he first decided on what branch of guitar playing most called out to him. He could have been a rhythm guitarist, a lead guitarist, a blues man, a Travis picker, he had dozens of options. Mayer decided that he wanted to be a finger picker, a lead guitarist with a folk/acoustic/jazz background. In other words, given his inherited whammy, Mayer picked the hardest path.

He started to practice, day in day out. Like a mad man he practiced. He conquered chords, worked his hearing, memorized patterns, watched the beats, read biographies, went to class, got feedback…and he did all of that year in and year out.

He came to the realization that he could adapt chords by either playing them in seventh position or an inverted position. In both cases his huge hands would be beneficial, as they could stretch.

As for picking patterns, because he couldn't develop more speed and he was competing with players that could use all their fingers, what Mayer did was craft a hack. He created a workaround where he would pull at strings, hammer on others, and even use his thumb, not only to pick but to create a distinctive percussive sound.
He did all of this through years of experimenting and practicing. Through years of jotting down where he was coming up short and, above all, through years of

following a plan. He did all of this not by constantly running to a wall and banging his head against it in order to break it, but by diligently chipping at key parts of said wall. He studied the structural plan and decided to approach his problems strategically.

Mayer created a framework based on what made a great guitar player. He studied up on his inspirations. He drew from their passions. He adapted that curriculum to his unique circumstances.

> *"One of the hardest things was tackling pieces I knew were way out of my league. Pieces I was aware I wasn't up to the challenge yet. I would practice each day. Each day something different that actually went hand in hand with my passion and goals, and then I would hit those pieces for at least half an hour. It was incredibly frustrating. Sometimes I simply felt like I wasn't even improving. Like all my work was a waste of time... Finally, one day, I started seeing an improvement. I started seeing that I could play those pieces, and not just place them but improvise on them."*

Now, here's another reason why I used John Mayer...he has a HUGE EGO, and having one (big or small) is pivotal to making it big.

5
YOU GOT ONE HELL OF AN EGO

"The passion for stretching yourself and sticking to it, even (or especially) when it's not going well, is the hallmark of a growth mindset. This is the mindset that allows people to thrive during some of the most challenging times in their lives."

Carol S. Dweck, author of *Mindset: The New Psychology of Success*

E go: A person's sense of self-esteem or self-importance.

You need to be extremely confident in your ability to perform.

You need self-esteem when there's nobody around.

You need to be able to learn on yourself during the tough times and tell yourself, "I got this."

This one of the key features of highly successful people that some people might not like. Their egos. Every single successful person has one hell of an ego. Some show it outwardly to the world, while others keep it to themselves when it is just as big. They're the type of people that are so confident in whatever it is that they do best that they pump themselves up and have an entire stadium in their mind cheering themselves on. That, my friends, is an ego. And though there are several books that talk about how ego should be the enemy, the most successful people don't bite that one bit.

Some of them are deluded monsters, with out-of-proportion egos and a mindset that basically tells them they can do no wrong and mountains were made to be conquered. When they look at Everest, they don't doubt that they'll climb to the top; they're too busy picking a cool parka for the Instagram photo and wondering if they can urinate at the peak and claim it as their own. These are cases in which the ego is outwardly expressed through foolish behavior, but hey, if that person is that confident in their ability and willing to look stupid, at least they'll be successful alone, right?

A great example of this emotional mind-game and mindset can be found in the biography of Steve Jobs. When Jobs was kicked out of Macintosh, he didn't blame his decision-making, not in a million years, for that colossal setback. He blamed the Board and called them tiny-minded neanderthals. He went and formed his own little company and basically started flicking Microsoft off. He was fueled by spite and the certainty that he was the technological messiah the world had been waiting for. People hated his blunt attitude but he cultivated a peculiar air.

"He's brilliant…because otherwise he's just an asshole."

That's not a quote I made up, but of an actual personal friend of Steve Jobs. He was labeled a tech guru not because he was smarter, but because of the way he carried himself. His followers needed to believe in his superiority because otherwise, they would have sacrificed so much for so little; not for a second could they conceive that they had been hailing a madman with a Napoleon complex.

Jobs' level of commitment into thinking that he was God's gift to technology and his gigantic ego can be easily illustrated in the following example:

Macintosh rehires Jobs after the former debacle and he instantly rebrands it as Apple. His first order of business was to make PCs and Laptops sexy again. Up until that point, IBM was shelling out great slabs of utilitarian machinery straight out of a communist labor camp. They were drab, they were colorless, bulky and crappy-looking.

To put it into context, Marc Maron - brilliant stand-up comic - once said:

> *"You marry an Apple. It's sexy, virginal, sanitized... But you cheat with a PC. It's old, dirty, full of bugs, and filled with your porn stash. You never put porn on an Apple; it's undignified."*

Anyway, Jobs promises the Board that he's going to relaunch the brand. He goes all fire and brimstone on their asses, calls them out on their lack of imagination, and promises to reinvigorate the brand. Moses coming down from Sinai and breaking the tablets on the idolaters' head. They get behind Jobs and basically give him a blank check.

"He seems to know what he's doing," they go. *"That man will lead us to the finish line."* Jobs is basically manhandling them and chastising them for their lack of imagination. He's drilling into their heads the fact that their old foggy ways bankrupted Macintosh. He's slapping them across the meeting room, lording over them the truism that he's the digital Second Coming and they are just a bunch of pigeon-brained twits. He's doing all of this and they are lapping it up. Nodding their heads and happily taking the dressing down.

Then, Jobs butters them up. Gives them a pie-in-the-sky ideal of what Apple can become. He starts flinging half-baked ideas.

"Man," they go, *"he's so sure of himself! We really are a bunch of idiots. That man knows his stuff!"*

They clap for him and give him complete control over Apple. Off he goes, the great Jobs…he calls his cronies, gives them the scoop, and they all ask:

"And how the heck are we going to pull that off? You said we'd have it done in six months? Are you mad? We don't even have a plan? None of what you promised can be done."

Jobs looks at all of them, smiles, and simply goes: *"Don't worry, it's easy. Trust me."*

They blink and something overcomes them… Like a snake charmer, Jobs confidence sparks something in them.

"Yeah, we will recreate the future! We will revolutionize the industry!" The battlecry goes up.

The day they launch Apple's new line - those translucent buckets from the start of this millennium with all those cool colors - Jobs goes onstage, in front of the world, and gives a legendary keynote address. He blindsides the world and Apple stock goes through the roof. Everyone in the planet now wants an Apple.

But, and here's the thing...THEY DIDN'T WORK as they should.

You Deluded F&%K

That's right, Jobs sold the world smoke. He sold the world a pretty little package, a nice-looking design, but a product that hadn't been completed...and a product that was full of bugs; the operating system, just to name one aspect, was a joke.
But all his employees knew, because Jobs drilled it into them through his own delusion, that they were going to meet that deadline. That the product, somehow, was going to work. Jobs' whole business strategy was based on his ego. All of his strategy was based off the two brass balls swinging by his legs and everyone thinking that he knew something they didn't.

But how, at the end of the day, did Jobs manage to construct Apple into the giant it is now? Because he was one deluded genius. He never once doubted that he could pull it off. He never once doubted that he was the best. He never once showed any lack of faith in his abilities. He was all conviction. Full of confidence. All ego.

"Ish, I'm confused. Chapter 1 was about knowing yourself. Being self-aware. Chapter 5 is about lying to yourself? One minute you're telling me to be self-aware. The next you're talking about being self-delusional."

Nope. Stick with me here - it will all make sense in a minute.

The Science Of Self Delusion

"Well, I think in a word: perseverance. Under the right conditions, if you're able to deceive yourself, it's what keeps you going. There's an old line that there are no atheists in foxholes, and I think that has broader application to self-deception. If when the going gets tough you're able to fool yourself into thinking things will work out, there can be an upside to this, and it's actually measurable, quantifiable, and can improve your performance in given situations… Across the board, studies show that the vast majority of college students overestimate their GPAs. They tend to remember every A they ever got, but if the grades go down, their memory gets worse. So, for instance, the recall rate for As was 89 percent, but for Bs it was only 29 percent. Even in their recent memories, students believed they were better students than they actually were. I went up to the attic and pulled out my own report card from the fifth grade. I had remembered myself as an A and B student, and there in my report card was a C+. And it was in writing, of all things. If I had gone through life believing I was a C+ writer, I'd probably have a different career path than the one I chose. Deceiving yourself about your own performance can actually have good benefits."

Joseph T. Hallinan,
Pulitzer Prize Winner and former *Wall Street Journal* reporter

Science as a whole has determined a few interesting things:

1. Being self-deluded, to a certain extent, in key areas is a great moral booster and actually helps in the whole self-awareness process. Yes, we will discuss this contradictory word salad further on.
2. Self delusions actually rewrite your synaptic centers (I'll explain this in the section to follow).
3. People have unconscious sensors that actually pick up on a person's ego… and not only that, they actually respond favorably to self-delusion and register it as confidence. And Confidence is king.

"In general, we are brands," psychologist Ian Wright told reporters of *The New York Times*, *"and as brands we sell ourselves constantly. We hide certain key aspects and reinforce others. And, above all, we adapt each time a new narrative - sort of like a marketing company - takes the wheel of our brand. But the one key aspect we can't lose sight of is the fact that we constantly have to present ourselves, us as a brand and product, in a strong valuable way."*

I often feel the heavy weight of imposter syndrome. Especially as a person of color working in tech, where Latino representation across the industry is between 4-8%.[6] It can be shattering to your confidence when you're in a room with a hundred other people and MAYBE there are a handful who look like you and come from a similar background, have similar interests, etc. Again, I'm able to get through this by tapping into that self-confidence, self-importance, and self-esteem. I remind myself things like "You've worked your ass off to be here. There's no reason why you don't deserve this. Now chin up and give them

---

[6] https://www.wired.com/story/five-years-tech-diversity-reports-little-progress/.

your best version of you." And if that is too much ego for you, then that's okay; search and find what works for you.

Confidence Is King

What do James Woods, Geena Davis, and Nolan Gould (the Dunphy Kid from *Modern Family*) have in common? Also, it's okay if you don't know who each of these people is - I found out about when I was knee deep in some research.

Okay, back to the point. They are all members of an almost secret society of geniuses known as MENSA. They also stand on shaky ground, almost quicksand-like soil, concerning their careers.

Each can solve a Rubik's Cube in a blink of an eye, yet somehow Howard Stern – with his 99 IQ – is remembered with greater respect and esteem.

The first three, like hundreds more, are prime examples of the fact that a high IQ doesn't necessarily equal success. They are test subjects that prove that a few more neurons don't make a lick of difference out in the real world.

The given fact that fools are the real movers and shakers of reality is a long since discovered certainty. The lead dancers are mostly idiots who can't properly tie a shoelace yet they somehow garner a meet-and-greet with the Dalai Lama. Many are individuals who trample on the very notion of intelligence, sound judgment, and good sense – and suddenly find themselves ordering their newly acquired staff to wipe down the Oval Office windows.

Ego Is Queen

The smartest person in the room, somehow overshadowed, and perhaps deep in the payroll, plays second fiddle to a great big lummox, wearing a beer-can helmet. This is a sad fact most of us face whenever we see a Kardashian on the television.

In a series of experiments conducted at Goldsmith University in London, a team of wise scientists proved what any teen in high school knows to be law:

Children with high confidence received the best marks at school regardless of their intellectual circumstances.

"There has been a very, very big lobby within educational psychology against the notion of IQ," notes psychologist Chamorro-Premuzic.

A list of factors constantly hampers all the momentum of the geniuses in the group to actually get to the finish line first:

Forward projection, thinking a few steps ahead, renders most people into fits of inactivity. What might be hailed as a cherished and coveted ability in chess is nothing short of debilitating in real life.

Further, Intellectual Coefficient (IQ) isn't the only thing that makes success. A series of data inputs ingrained within us somehow go to town on our general matrix. One smidgen of sand, in any category, determines the way we act or function with the outside world. Behind every letter of the alphabet there is a Q besides it. EQ, Emotional; MQ, Moral; SQ, Sexual; GQ, Gentlemen's Quarterly.

All these types of intellects fundamentally drive us towards or away from success. The right measure and balance equals a respectful, tepid asshole. One pinch in any of the Q columns, and you suddenly shift into the epic asshole category.

With me so far?

IQ might render us sterile when trying to accomplish a task. Confidence is the proverbial rocket sparking a light on our ass.

This is a huge finding. It may seem the sort of thing that doesn't move planets, but in hindsight and upon further inspection, it might very well dictate policy around the world.

Everyone has a friend, top of their class, valedictorian, who can solve complex equations while doing a Sudoku puzzle, but can't seem to get their shit together. The one who never amounts to anything and is a constant disappointment. "You have so much potential..."

Then, on the other side of the tracks, you have another buddy who flies by the seat of his pants, who goes headlong into a fire half naked with a towel wrapped around his head, who believes that being ill-prepared is all good... Who, for all logical reason, should be in a grave, but somehow not only lands on his feet but manages to rack up victory after victory. It's not luck, or serendipity, or irony; it's confidence.

Confidence is strength and it will allow you to make the tough or unpopular choices when necessary. It is the sort of factor that, psychologists will tell you, makes stubborn monkeys out of all of us. And, interestingly enough, it is just this attitude that ultimately separates the herd.

It allows you to double down, particularly when you're ahead. It permits you to sell an idea as a reality. It bypasses your genetic and intellectual limitations and makes you bulletproof. It allows you to accept help when needed, whereas the scholarly arrogance and those certain on their brainy superiority may be blind to the tools others bring to the table – conglomerates, employers, and even sexual partners.

Doing something with aplomb, panache, and style is far more important than doing it well.

Be Batman

Have you ever heard of the super hero pose?

Be Batman. There's something about the dark knight. He's appealing to all genres.

There's a general idea, as far as superheroes are concerned, that Batman is basically the big badass of the whole bunch. And in part of the great attraction of the character. Batman is what every living person, us mortals, can strive to. He's the man who kicked Superman's ass! There's this book that came out a while ago called *Train like Batman*, or something like that. What's really cool about it is that it shows you a physical and mental routine that can actually help you become Batman.

So, like they say:

If you can be anyone, be yourself, unless you can be Batman...always be Batman.[7]

Hands on the hips, elbows out, chin up, chest out – a pose that establishes dominance and tells the world you're the boss. Studies done by the University of Michigan have established that certain poses create an actual positive reaction in people.

One of the most interesting is the superhero pose.

Just 10 to 15 seconds in front of a mirror, daily, actually helps boost confidence levels in the long and short run. Many great CEOs and political figures actually practice this right before a big meeting.

But why am I going on about Batman?

Because that little mental routine is based on an actual neurological experiment conducted by Harvard on confidence boosting.

---

[7] Can you tell I was a big Batman fan growing up and dressed up as him for about 10 Halloweens? Anyway, back to the example…

The Science of the Dark Knight

Psychological researchers have come to a wild, mind-blowing revelation. The superhero stance – that iconic pose – Superman and the like determinedly practiced in the mirror. The stance of "Shoot me, I dare you. 'Cause I'm the boss. Bullets bounce off me, and I don't even bat an eye." That look – chest puffed out, chin facing skyward, the determined glare of an enraged fan, legs spread apart and fists clenched up against your hips – cannot only make you feel and act differently. It can actually alter your hormonal output. I'm not making this up, it's science.

A research team– with too much coffee and comics in their midst – came up with this hypothesis. The experiment was multifaceted, with dozens of participants, mixed and-matched. It had everything. Gambling, posturing, alpha and beta male square-offs, maybe even fist fights. I won't bore you with the medical heavy details, but once the small environment of participants and the experimenters, filled with excitement from what they had just witnessed during the trials, dispersed, the awesome revelations fell like a hammer over cartoon heads.

Saliva samples were taken, blood tests were analyzed, and shrinks rated each human guinea pig. The results? Those that acted like superheroes, those that felt they were powerful masks of themselves, beat out the wimpy sample group in absolutely every test.

The superheroes were willing to assume more risks. They were unconsciously more open to relationships. And, far more startling, their brains actually short circuited. They were inundated with countless different hormones.

Testosterone levels rose right on the spot and continued for 17 minutes after the stance. The prevailing theory is that the brain can't differentiate between the potential of power – or the idea – and actual power.

But that wasn't all, Cortisol – sometimes referred to as "stress hormone" – actually decreased. With time, those individuals who practiced the superhero pose could actually alter their cortisol baseline. In other words, after a while, they actually managed to develop an immunity to it. The general summation: "Stand like a superhero, act like a superhero."

Under Armour was the first to realize the marketing potential. They created and made millions out of their unique Alter Ego line. They evolved from simple hero logos on their compression shirts to limited edition apparel based on that summer's big action movie. They made fitted, muscle-hugging, tight tees, perfectly balanced for your performance. These T-shirts, mind you, are based on your favorite characters. Under Armour isn't the only one. A quick browse on Amazon will reveal a world of possibilities. From long-sleeved – bionic arm – Winter Soldier T-shirts to belly-hugging Deadpool T-shirts, each is designed for all training purposes.

And you want to know what they discovered? That it actually helped athletes' performances. A shirt actually upped their games. Yes, it might be self delusion, because they were certainly not jumping over tall buildings in a single bound, but at a chemical response level, and biological one at that, they were outperforming their old marks. More hormonal output, more crank in the way their muscle groups responded.

Want to lift weights like the Hulk? Run around the National Mall like Wonder Woman? Show everyone at the gym that you are Thor? Well, thankfully, you are living in the golden era of: "Simply take my money and shut up!" Improve your performance, your speed, your overall attitude, with these possibilities. Like I said, "Be Batman!"

The Value of Self Talk

"Talk to yourself like you would to someone you love."

Brené Brown

Our brain is hardwired to act on motivational speeches. There's no getting around it. On a purely chemical level, we react positively to key words and if those words are twisted and primed in such a manner as to demand an action, our hormonal system starts pumping to release the right cocktail.

All those inspirational quotes, speeches, high fives and verbal mind games that constantly assail us and make us feel invincible are basically formulas that trigger hormonal responses in our brain. Psychologically speaking, these battlecries are nothing more than hacks. Some might be corny, some might be idiotic, some might even make little too no sense, but in essence our brain - at an instinctual level - doesn't really care. Our brain doesn't take apart that quote or the nonsense or the hipster-primed directive and put it under the microscope, nope. Our brain reacts to a phrase's key components.

Scientists have linked this behavior to music.

For as long as there has been sound in the universe and humans have been able to process it, we've linked certain noises to deep emotional responses. The growl of a tiger, the trickle of a waterfall, the laughter of a child…these, plus millions more stimuli, poke our cerebral cortex and evoke memories or intense reactions or even evolutionary red flags. It is a strange phenomena that allows us to access different mental states and emotional spaces in the blink of an eye.

The reason for these sensations was partly discovered by a study conducted by the Montreal Neurological Institute and Hospital. Certain sounds, at a purely vibrational scale, cause a massive physical reaction. One chord, say a G chord, because of the notes used, can actually create tangible and sudden onsets of emotions, which in turn are followed by an actual physical reaction of the body. Why those particular notes? Because years of evolution have hardwired our brain into associating those notes with pleasure and bliss. Their strident and sharp report, on an auditory level, is very similar to natural sounds linked to pleasure, bliss, and fun.

On the other end of the spectrum, notes on the minor scale - due to their similarity with natural sounds associated with danger - instantly cause us to be on edge or depressed.

Using brain imaging, the Montreal Neurological Institute and Hospital determined which mix and match of notes triggers different neurotransmitters in our brain. They determined, without a shadow of a doubt, that songs like "Happy" by Pharrell, and other tunes within that musical compass, release large amounts of dopamine, the hormone responsible for pleasure, confidence, positive self-esteem and joy… At a purely chemical level, whenever we hear "Happy," along with thousands of other songs within that spectrum, our bodies experience hormonal discharge as if we were in the throes of sex, food, or drugs.

Well, other scientists actually took that study and ran with it. They started to investigate other fields associated with brain mapping and what other things, subtle cues at a sensory level, actually stimulated different areas of our brains and unleashed certain hormonal gates. What colors, for example, we evolutionarily - at a purely instinctual level - associate with happiness, sadness, confidence, sex, violence, death, money, obsession. What facial expressions, gestures, and other visual cues, such as body language, are associated with different neurotransmitters. What clothes we instinctually link to power, to poverty, to relaxing, or to rebellion. And like those million of other minuscule cues that we as humans don't analyze, but our brain does, due to Darwin's process and catalogues.

All of this takes us back to verbal cues.

An examination backed by various studies and programs determined that most inspirational quotes actually followed a simple subroutine or formula. And that very formula, if carefully followed, actually produces a tangible and physical reaction in our brain. In other words, like a wizard casting a spell, if we hear certain words in a certain procession, we can actually feel a neurological response and physical reaction within us.

Most of these speeches and inflamed motivational quotes are composed of key words, strung together around an action verb in a simple manner with a repeating pattern if it's more than a sentence long. 'You are the change you want to see in the world' is a clear example. It gives the listener the idea that they are incredibly important and builds the inspirational bullet around two sentences, both cemented on verbs linked up by the same pronoun, YOU. It's effective because it's simple and uses that key pronoun as a beat. Most quotes, at least those that are remembered, are constructed with this pattern in mind. They are demands, calls to action.

And, as with "Happy," we little cogs respond instinctually to these repeating patterns. We're hardwired to feel joy, confidence, pleasure, and elation in response to the right set of verbal commands.

Most successful people know this at an instinctual level. They are constantly rallying around a battlecry - "I got this," "Just do it," "You're worthy," "Today is going to be a good day," "You deserve this," - to hack their mindset. They know the value of a good personal cheerleading squad. People like: Jim Carrey, Denzel Washington, Jennifer Lopez, Oprah Winfrey, Christian Bale, and hundreds more.

> *"I dedicate around 15 minutes a day to affirmations, to building myself up. This industry is cruel and tough and you have to stay strong and positive in order to succeed. They help me feel grateful, grounded and ambitious."*
>
> Jennifer Lopez,
> Actress, singer, dancer, fashion designer, producer, and businesswoman

Can you have a huge EGO and also be humble?

Yes, as long as the ego is controlled and there are people in your life to check you when it's getting out of hand.

Ish's Affirmations

A few constant reminders that I live by:

Your family didn't sacrifice all that they did for you to give up now.
Keep going.
By doing this, you're paving the way for someone else to learn
and grow as well.
Your purpose is to help others achieve their goals.

Sayings that I literally tell myself aloud or in my head on a daily basis:

You got this.
Push through.
X more reps, come on, you can do it.
Concentrate.
Focus.
Relax.
Breathe.
Keep going.
Make an impact.

Affirmations:

You deserve this.
You are worthy.
Be humble.

You will be successful if you work at it.
Be yourself.
Be grateful.

People I listen to when I need to be uplifted:

Eric Thomas
Brené Brown
Will Smith
Les Brown
My parents
My grandparents

6
EYES ON THE PRICE

No matter where you're headed, you need a goal. An endpoint. Something you can cling to and call the end of your journey…even if that journey turns out like one of those standalone movies:

"Just a great film… No franchise… No sequel… Let's just make a great film."

Executives after the opening weekend: "Screw that, this is breaking the Box office… Make a sequel ASAP!"

That's a different way of saying: your goal doesn't necessarily have to be set in stone; it can adapt, become flexible, even transform into something different altogether. Nonetheless, the key to success is to have a goal, to actually start walking or planning a path with, at the very least, a destination in sight. So far we've broken down the very foundations of who you are by comprehending the idea of self-concept, and getting some insight into what makes each and every one of us tick. Adapted our patterns, behaviors, and habits to that true concept of US. Understanding the necessity of learning and knowledge, and fortifying our foundations by feeding our grey matter. We've walked through the jagged forest of putting in the work and getting lost in the repetition of exercise. And finally, we've crashed headlong into the iceberg called Ego and understood that it's not necessarily a bad thing. Now, it's time to sit down, take a deep breath, and come to the realization that all of what we're doing, and what's left of this book, is towards a specific ideal, towards something. We are doing this with an end in sight…and it's time to identify what it is.

The Reality of Goals

"People don't really know what they want. That's the truth. In this business, everyone wants to be a director, or an actor, or a scriptwriter, that's it. Those are the 3 outs they have. You're either one of those or you call it quits. In reality, movie making is a huge endeavor, made by thousands of ingenious and rather plucky individuals. They each have their value and they each have a part to play."

That's Sam Mendes right there. The director of *American Beauty*, and the last three or so James Bond films. Sam Mendes later went on to stipulate some of the harsh realities of the biz. Primarily he makes it a point to highlight the fact that what drives many folks' ambitions and desires into breaking it into Hollywood is ignorance. Ignorance into not only what it means, but ignorance as to the possibilities at hand.

What most people conceptualize as a director is a fallacy. There's this Howard Hughes, Stanley Kubrick ideal of a man or woman with a camera framing scenes and making everything fall seamlessly into place. A godlike being, standing over his set snapping toys together and barking out orders to his crew. In reality, a director is just that, someone who directs - he has a very flimsy vision of what he wants and an astonishingly creative and professional team that does most of the heavy lifting. He or she reads the script - interprets a very rough interpretation of how everything should come out - and then they call their war council only to receive the following response:

"That will not work...how about we do this instead?"

The actors will butt heads with them on how they believe the character should behave. The cinematographer will reinterpret frames, lens, and light set-ups, the editor will grab their product and mix and match it at their own discretion, the producers will finagle the end result in conjunction with focus groups. In the end, during the whole shot, the director will most likely just find himself sitting on a chair, looking at a screen while his whole crew works to fulfill a composite vision.

The scriptwriter. In most cases they are nothing more than a freelancer of hired contractors that get paid per project and never really make their way onto a set. Their job starts once they get a call from a producer telling them to prepare a script based on someone else's outline and ends the second their paycheck is deposited and they hand in the script, months from pre-production.

All of this is simply to illustrate what Sam Mendes was trying to convey: educate yourself before committing to a dream. Sometimes it might not be exactly what you think it is. You might think you want to be a director, but in reality, what you aspire and what really flames your passion are the technical aspects of movie making; the cameras, the lenses, the science behind it. You might be deadset on making it as a scriptwriter, but maybe your desires are more in line with those of an executive producer, the person that oversees the narrative and the general storyline.

In most key industries, and most high-end glamorous business, the jobs that really trend are the flashy ones, the simple ones, the ones that end up on Instagram, or the ones that win the awards. When you see Taylor Swift receiving her Grammys and whatnots, you fail to capture that string of names she's spouting off and thanking for all her success, each one key to the brand that is Swift. And each one as influential as she, only working behind the curtain, so to speak.

Everyone remembers Elton John, yet they seem to forget Bernie Taupin. A famous story about the Elton legend occurred in an airport minutes from the Rocketman's departure to the States. The airplane he was on was grounded, on special request. The hatch sprung open, and in came John Lennon. Lennon, it turns out, had jettisoned onto the runway and begged the pilot to hit the brakes. Anyhow, one of the Beatles boarded Elton's plane, went up to Mr. "Yellow Brick Road," and said:

> *"Thank you, I think 'Your Song' is by far the best anthem of this generation. It's simply amazing. The lyrics are magical..."*

Elton turned to Lennon and said, "You're on the wrong plane. Thanks, but Bernie Taupin is who you should be talking to."

Who's Taupin, you ask? He's basically the writer of almost every Elton John song. Taupin is basically the poet who made Elton. And like him, only a handful of people actually know who he is.

So, when you're setting up your goals, it's important to simply sit back and actually take stock of what they are. Why you're winning them up and fighting for them. Why? Because most of the time, as most successful people will tell you, your dreams, your passions don't really align with what you think is your objective. You don't need to be Taylor Swift in order to break bank, make millions, and be part of the music industry. You don't need to be Elton John to make pop history. You don't need to be Sam Mendes to be part of a James Bond movie. You don't need to be a Steve Jobs to change the modern world. You don't need to be Warren Buffet to move markets.

All you really need is to understand what it is you want. What it is that drives you towards that objective.

The Fatalist Feature

One of the key features about setting goals and actually achieving them is that science has determined that we have to be fatalistic about the whole endeavor. Fatalism, as a practice, is nothing short of the middle ground between pessimism and optimism.

The **pessimist** sees the glass half full: "Ugh, I need more water! We are all going to die. How can I make it with just that little bit of water?"

The **optimist** looks at the glass: *"Oh, man that's a ton of water. We'll be good for weeks."*

The **fatalist** looks at the glass: *"Well, that's all the water we have. Don't get your panties in a bunch, there's nothing we can do. Let's make a plan and start to ration it. You, over there, got any ideas of where to get more water?"*

Did you spot the difference? The pessimist is paralyzed by the uncertainty of the future, by the possibility that everything is one bad day away from going tipsy and ending in a calamity. In a zombie movie, the pessimist would be a LEVEL 1 kill…the person that gets picked off right from the start because they can't handle the dire straits. The optimist meanwhile is chipper to a "T," hoping that water will appear, and really doesn't do anything to make it so. In a zombie movie, he's a LEVEL 2 kill… Everyone loves their infectious, *"Everything is going to be okay."* The fatalist meanwhile is a LEVEL 9 kill…he's Daryl from *The Walking Dead* or Woody Harrelson from *Zombieland*. They're making plans, storming the gun shop, getting a copy of the *Anarchist Cookbook*, teaching everyone survival skills and, in a coldhearted fashion, analyzing the Apocalypse and cooking up a gameplay.

To reach your goals, to even make a goal, neurobiology and psychology have determined that you need to be a fatalist – the person that sees the glass for what it is and makes a plan from that tangible reality.

Fantasizing about your goal, thinking that you will get it no matter what, is actually detrimental to achieving it. It robs you of motivation. Our brain, as we've covered so many times in this book, is an easy mark. It's incredibly simple to scam it. Constantly thinking and imagining yourself already at the finish line, with your goal safely tucked inside your pocket, actually tricks the brain into thinking that you have already achieved said objective. You brain no longer needs to pump your with hormones, chemicals, and goal efficient scenarios because, to it, you already accomplished what you desired.

Meanwhile, always contemplating on the fact that your objective is a daunting feat, that it is something unattainable, also shuts down your brain. Your brain, like every part of your being, has a hardwired survival instinct. It classifies everything as a potential life-ending threat. *"Ahh,"* you say. *"I'm never going to get that body. Look at those abs. It's impossible. I'm genetically predisposed to always have a gut. Why even try? Should I go to the gym?"* You brain's response: *"DANGER! Why is my host so negative towards the gym? Dear God, we're going to die in the gym! Don't go! Stay at home, binge watch Netflix... EAT HOT CHEETOS! They are still walking towards the bag... code red, pump them with neurotransmitters...bring their mood down."*

Meanwhile, your brain likes a challenge and that's exactly what a fatalist presents to it.

Personally speaking, I'm definitely a fatalist first, and optimist second.
I think through options a, b, c, d, and e, for situations – the worst case scenario, the best case scenario, the odds, the different variables, and what I need to do to achieve the desired outcome. Then I take all of this and build a plan and put on my optimistic hat while executing, knowing that I've already thought of five other alternatives in case things change. And if for some reason something comes up that I didn't plan for, I know that I can remain calm under pressure to make the best possible decision given the situation. I really do hate pessimism and I don't like being around pessimistic people. Keep your negativity to yourself. If you've got valid feedback, I'm all ears, but don't be negative just for the sake of having nothing better to contribute to the situation.

When a fatalist sees a problem, they instinctually have a need to solve it. They see the bad, the good, and the ugly. Studies have shown fatalists suffer from what is called "The Endowment Effect."

The Endowment Effect

In a nutshell, the Endowment Effect is referred to in human studies as the action of taking something, labeling it as *"ours,"* and then integrating it into our sense of identity. This is the reason why we go crazy when the neighbor's dog steps onto our lawn. It is a survival trait that we inherited from our ancestors - the hunter/gatherers - when they decided to quit their nomadic ways and crop the fields and claim the land.

Researchers at Cornell University demonstrated the effect with a clever experiment. They gave various participants coffee mugs and offered to trade them chocolate for their mugs; almost none took the candy.

"Maybe they really liked their mugs. Some are pretty cool."

Those same researchers then got another control group and reversed the trial. Now they gave their human lab rats chocolate bars and this time they asked the participants if they were willing to trade their chocolate bars for the fancy mugs. Very few took the deal.

It wasn't about the object, per se; it was about the fact that they had taken ownership of said object. This happens to all of us. When we have that one mug at work that's ours and only ours. When we go to school and always sit in the same chair. When we go to sleep on one side of the bed, even when it's completely empty. When we simply can't throw away that worn-out pair of jeans, even though they are about to fall apart.

When we take ownership of something, we work to keep it. It becomes part of our personality.

Fatalists, above all, have a way of taking ownership of the SITUATION. They become invested in the intangible more than the tangible. Most successful people can be easily classified as fatalist on certain personality tests; they score high on that curve. That's why they are great leaders. That's why they step up and never step down. That's why they complete their goals. They link their identity, their *whole* identity, to that goal...they take ownership of it. Not just the good bits, but the bad as well. The inherent struggles said goal will inevitably create become intricate cogs in the way they perceive themselves. The joy of obtaining the goal also transforms into a baseline of their personality.

Creating Your Own Luck

Luck, that fickle crap. You may have the math down to a science, you might know the odds at a Blackjack table, but there's one thing you can never really control...CHAOS. The randomness of creation might be something science can generally calculate - statistics and all that - but in reality even they are stumped most of the time.

> *"You said the penny was going to come up heads... I paid you a trillion dollars to develop a machine to predict the outcome. Is that honest, Abe?!"*

Nowadays, we have millions of way to make educated guesses and anticipate possible outcomes. To craft a forecast of what might happen. But there's a reason why sometimes you're at the beach in your swimming trunks staring at a stormy sky while pissed off at the Weather Channel; life, nature, the cosmos are unpredictable. We call the crystal ball smashing trick LUCK or FATE.

Some people believe that they have been so unfortunate to be born under a bad sign. No matter what they do, they seem to never get a break and constantly be hit with "bad luck." But, and here's the first thing you have to ask yourself: IS THERE SUCH A THING AS LUCK?

The Science of Luck

Some people seem to turn everything they touch into gold; others meanwhile are constantly harassed by misfortune. From a purely logical and physical (there are no such things as leprechauns and pots of gold at the end of the rainbow) perspective, there really is no such thing as luck.

Luck is simply a perfectly reasonable way of highly creative people to talk about how things might have easily turned out. It isn't a property, like mass, or weight, or an object.

There are two spectrums of science that debate the existence of luck. The only branch of physics that can remotely say that "maybe," "perhaps," "might," and so forth exist are those that have a very loose interpretation of quantum mechanics. This branch says that someone or something that knows enough about the universe and its laws should be entirely capable of predicting - in principle - the outcome of absolutely everything. It is called physical determinism. But it's not LUCK, but the understanding that everything, with enough foreknowledge, can be predicted; that casualty doesn't exist and every action is partially deterministic.

If this is even remotely true, then it undermines free will and moral responsibility. No matter what we do, no matter what we think, no matter what we might want, the UNIVERSE, from a physics standpoint, has already planted a course for us and we're just puppets to its whims. If science were ever to prove that, then our society would devolve into chaos; just for a second, think of all the implications. America, for example, would stop being the land of the free...because, in essence, we're not. Next time they catch someone standing over a body, bloodied and guilty, they could easily get off by invoking: "Science says it's not my fault...fate made me do it."

Luckily, this is just a small branch of quantum physics - the fringe group. In reality most scientists have proven to a certain degree that reality is simply "indeterministic"; it is impossible to predict everything no matter how much you know. Here are my thoughts on luck:

> *"If something good happens to us once, then it is luck. If it happens to us often, then it is skill. There's this old saying, lighting can't strike twice, when in reality it can. Some places, due to their location and geological content, attract more lighting than other places. Some people also, for various biological reasons, attract more lighting than others. If you place someone with this proneness and have them hanging around a thunderstorm with those qualities, then they will be a lot more likely to be struck by lighting. Was it that they were unlucky? Or was it simply that they were uninformed about certain facts? Luck is something closely linked to fate and destiny, once you get to know certain things about reality you slowly understand that those concepts don't really exist. Conversely, you can actually manufacture your own "luck" if you know what you're doing and do your research."*

If luck is just that, the cheap lucky rabbit's foot we hang our hopes and dreams on, the one we bought at the gas station, then why try to harness it? It's like trying to bottle magic, when Harry Potter comes up to you and says, *"It's all a scam, man. The wand? Made by Apple. All you really need is good WiFi."* Because, even if it doesn't exist, there's still a part of us that believe in the fairytale of it.

> *"Most scientists nowadays are atheist, but a great majority of those were raised in very religious backgrounds. As a psychologist I can tell you that this dichotomy often brings them troubling issues."*
>
> Margaret Biner, PhD

You might not believe in luck, but that doesn't mean that it won't influence you on a cerebral and unconscious level. We are slaves to our backgrounds. We might know that the Force isn't real, but *Star Wars* fans can't help but smile every time a coincidence in their life reminds them of it, and we hope that we are wrong.

So, here are tips to help to hack your luck. Whether you believe in it or not, these steps will help you out either way.

1. Be Social.

Ivian Misner, in his book *Networking Like a Pro,* goes on long speeches on the importance of broadening your social circle to improve your odds. The best way to garner more luck is to collect more new acquaintances and to hack your profile, purely statistically.

Introduce old friends to new acquaintances. Galvanize and look for new connection…connections bring opportunities. Build stronger bonds with those friends you can rely on.

As you become more social and build your networks, remember to keep an eye and ear out for nuggets of knowledge. Learn from these people and take mental notes over time. Think back to compound learning from Chapter 3 — the more you pick up from them, the more you'll improve your "luck" in future situations.

2. Visualize.

Fatalists, for the most part, are walking, talking computers. They have a knack for reverse-engineering. In a calm and orderly fashion, they visualize the path to success and figure out how to obtain their goals by working backwards.

In cold and often frightening clarity, they look at the endgame and start to walk away from it, perfectly jotting down every detail and setback they see along that route until they arrive back to the present. They are futurist, seeing each hurdle, each hiccup, each battle, and writing it down.

The key to success is to be honest and see the world as it is, not as how you wish it could be. Bring each detail and each mountainside along the way to your objective in high resolution

3. Randomness.

Let the unexpected grant you new perspective.

Here's the thing – most successful people get bored and stifled and they sometimes need to visit their neighbors and crack open a bottle of Mezcal and simply have some fun.

Our brain needs to forgo control and every so often allow the creative hemisphere to take over. Turing, Churchill, Descartes, Gates, every artist out there, has often detailed how incredibly powerful this has been for their career. They later say it was fate or serendipity, but in actuality it was simply a moment where their creative hemisphere gave them a jolt of inspiration. It allowed them to think outside the box. Something as simple as using your non-dominant hand for half an hour for absolutely everything, like brushing your teeth, cooking, writing, etc., can actually help you access this state; from a neurological point of view, an action like that tricks the logical hemisphere and makes it stand aside.

4. Work Hard.

Psychologist Richard Wiseman has studied luck and its presence in people's lives. He found that if you think you'll be lucky, chances are you'll experience more good fortune than someone who thinks they are unlucky. About 82% of lucky people are prepared to work hard and create their good luck. They also have a positive attitude and are resilient when bad things happen.

Unlucky people tend to be cynical and believe that no matter how hard they work, they will be unlucky. As Wiseman notes, it becomes a self-fulfilling prophecy.

5. Accept Failure.

You don't fail, you succeed in finding what doesn't work. Each and every failure brings you closer to a future success if you're willing to learn from those experiences.

Instinct, Luck, or Something Else?

When we are faced with the wonders of technology and what new and exciting avenues it will afford humanity, we constantly fall into the same tired expression:

> *"My computer will never know how to express emotions, compose a musical hit, or ultimately do anything based on instinct alone."*

Computers are, in essence, relegated to the stratosphere of cold, unimaginative, data processing labs. The heart and soul of a person, that magical IT that guides us through life and allows us to make decision based on "gut feelings," are functions that a computer or A.I. will never be able to reproduce or copy.

We will always have an extra leg in that race, thanks to these fundamental characteristics of the human experience. A program will never have that ability; those instincts.

Well, time to burst that bubble... Science and neurologists have determined that not only can a computer function on "instincts" alone, but it can actually be more efficient at it. Furthermore, what we call "instinct," which in part is what fuels luck, can actually be taught. It is an acquired trait, nothing more.

You see, instinct, the ability to make brash and sudden decisions (and correct ones at that) based on a feelings or an emotional trigger, is in reality a complex neurological and chemical process. It's not fate. It's not a guardian angel. It's not a little voice in our head, put there by some being to guide us. It's just our brain, synapses, and neurons working over time and giving us advice at lighting-fast speed.

Research has determined that when we act on instinct, we are in fact acting on "Pattern Recognition." There really is no such thing as luck or instinct, just cold, hard calculation and probabilities. Our brain is analyzing thousands of inputs at once and then gifting us with a response based on that same analysis.

Let's take an overly successful business mogul. They go into a meeting, a one on one, and after some finagling and cut-throat negotiations, they come out having made a multi-million dollar trade agreement.

"How did you know when to ease up on the pressure? When to give the carrot and forestall the stick?" asks one of his hangers-on. *"How did you know the limit? That if you pushed a bit more, the deal would fall apart?"*
"Kid, I'm a pro. Been doing this for ages. You develop instincts after a while."

The mogul truly believes that they closed that gigantic handshake based on some sixth sense, but what really happened in that meeting was something a bit more complicated. After years of practice, the business mogul developed his senses. These senses noticed patterns and picked up things that they weren't even aware of. They detected body language, facial expressions, smells, the passage of time, the blood vessels bursting, the comfort level of the other person, and dozens upon dozens of other inputs. Then they compared those visual cues to other patterns they'd catalogued over the years, in similar situations, and gave the mogul a "feeling" on how to act. It wasn't luck, it wasn't a sixth sense, it was simply their brain doing its thing.

When you go into a bar and try to spit game at someone that you're attracted to, you're not working off instincts, you're not working off luck; you're employing pattern recognition. Your brain is analyzing potential mates – it's calculating probabilities based on what they are wearing, what they are drinking, the way they stand or sit, the way they lean against the bar or cross their legs, their eye movements, the cologne or perfume they are wearing, the pitch of their voice, the way they interact with others, whether they are smiling or not, and dozens of other visual clues. Then, when we stroll up to then, our brain is making logical leaps not based on intuition but based on logic and patterns. If we take that person home, or form a relationship, it wasn't because of instinct or luck; it was because our internal Sherlock Holmes was playing with the odds and probabilities and measuring the stats.

What scientists have determined is that computers can actually perform this function, this "instinctual" leap of faith, far better than human beings. They can do this because they have greater processing power. They can analyze a situation to a greater extent and with more stats available to form a satisfactory response. What scientists have also discovered is that this characteristic - that can be programmed into computers - can also be "programmed" into other people. In other words, folks can learn how to develop their "instincts."

A cursory internet search on "body language" will pop out thousands of articles and videos on the subject. FBI specialists training common folks on the subject.

Psychologists droning on and on about the merits of reading and understanding body language in order to get ahead in your chosen field or profession.

Another search on "fashion" and what it dictates in any given situation will also provide a ton of articles and videos on the topic. What a color says about a person's emotional state. What brands appeal to certain personality types. What a tie tells the observer. Is their shirt ironed? What does that mean?

Successful people can analyze all of these factors, and dozens more - smells, cologne, eye movement, even the person's moisture level and whether they are sweating or not - and make educated guesses on how to interact with that person. Then, HIGHLY successful people, those that are a rung or two above simply successful folks, not only analyze those factors but actually use patterns to fool and trick their opponents. They craft their appearances and their actions in order to solicit "instinctual" responses from the individual or group they are interacting with.

Take Steve Jobs. Yes, we've used him already but he's a caricature that everyone can remember. There was a reason why Steve always wore the same outfit…because it was unassuming, plain, and his brand. It was an outfit that said absolutely nothing about his intentions or his motivations. He was using his competitors' pre-suppositions and assumptions, as well as their pre-conceptions and own highly honed Pattern Recognitions skills, against them. He was robbing them of the one thing they had relied on for all their business ventures: THEIR INSTINCT. This action infused Steve with the mysterious – it elevated him into the mythical on account that his demeanor and outward appearance weren't quantifiable. It said nothing, absolutely nothing, about him. Everything you do, everything you wear, everything you say is a clue as to what makes you tick.

SMART Goals

Let's bring out the mnemonics, the acronyms, the memory devices. Let's bring out the ever efficient learning technique and construct a very cool acronym.

SMART is a guided way of setting up objectives and goals, an elaborative one-word construct, each letter highlighting a key factor in goal setting: Specific, Measurable, Attainable, Realistic, and Time-bound.

In November of 1981, George T. Doran published an article on Management Review. It was a careful examination of how to handle your ambitions and make targeted intentions in life you can actually obtain; in other words, how to designate mission parameters that are actually relevant and not pie-in-the-sky actions and aims.

The article was titled, "There's a S.M.A.R.T. way to write management's goals and objectives."

Ideally speaking, according to Doran, each corporation, department, and individual should devise their goals under criteria that quantified said objectives. That allowed the user to qualify on a scale every aspect of the goal. More importantly, it gifted the user a way to properly qualify whether or not an objective managed to efficiently complete its intended purpose.

Every Goal should encompass the following five factors:

1) Specific: It must be a niched goal, target specific and aimed at improving a designated area.

2) <u>Measurable</u>: You have to be able to qualify its progress.
3) <u>Assignable</u>: You have to be able to assign it to someone or something and, more to the point, a specific individual who in a way is tailor made for that goal.
4) <u>Realistic</u>: Given your available resources, be realistic. It should be something practical and sensible.
5) <u>Time-related</u>: You have to have a deadline, a specific amount of time the goal should be achieved in.

Doran later goes on to discuss that this is not a binding structure and it is in fact a fluid model. A great objective should be able to fill out those five key steps, BUT, depending on what you're trying to achieve, that might be a pipe dream. Certain goals don't adhere to all these rigorous factors…but they should, at the very least, comply with three of them in order to have a reasonable chance of becoming a reality.

Grab this year's New Year Resolution and say it out loud.

Notice something? That's right, it's very vague. It's very generic.

"Get in shape." "Earn more money." "Go on vacation." "Be a better parent." "Find love." "Get a promotion." "Buy a house." "Get pregnant." "Get organized." "Quit smoking." "Exercise more."

What do you notice now that you've been reading this chapter? That's right, these goals are extremely wide and sweeping. General and nonexclusive. Now, snatch any one from that list and faithfully apply the SMART model to their makeup; see them under that lens and adapt them to those criteria.

"Get in shape."

What do I consider as being in GOOD shape? Do I have a paradigm? Do I have a model? Do I want to be sexy or bring my cholesterol down? Do I want to just look good on the outside? How can I measure whether or not my efforts are paying off? Am I the right person for the job, or should I seek out professional help? What tools do I have at my disposal? Do I have the physical stamina, fortitude, or makeup for such a goal? How long do I think it should take?

There's a difference between getting in shape, having a healthy lifestyle, or simply looking good. Maybe you don't need to trim down your waist and your doctor already told you that you're fine; instead, you need to start eating better, as your blood sugar levels are high. Maybe you have a fast metabolism and you can't seem to build muscle. Maybe, when you say "get in shape," what you're really thinking is "look good," and a quick shopping-spree at ZARA with a fashion advisor can fix that up. Once you manage to focus your goal and individualize it, you can make it more deterministic because it applies to you, and you alone.

Let's use, for example, the most common interpretation of "Get in shape"… your belly is growing out of proportion and you've had take-out food three weeks straight.

S.M.A.R.T.

- Specific: "I need to lose some pounds. I'm overweight."
- Measurable: "Each week, my goals is X amount of pounds."
- Assignable: "It's something I need to do, but I also need a support group. I need a nutritionist to track my progress and help me out with food choices. I need a personal trainer for all that gym stuff. I need a therapist for the inevitable emotional avalanche all of this will bring. I need family members to encourage me."
- Realistic: "I don't have the time to eat healthy; there's a reason I always partake of those sinful chimichangas. I hate broccoli. Tuna tastes awful. I've never once gone out running and I get breathless going up the stairs. The closet gym is a 20-minute drive."
- Time-related: "I need to get fit for my summer vacations. That's six months."

See how a good-natured phrase such as "Get in shape" suddenly transformed itself into a battle plan? Now you have a path set before you with stiff deadlines and a weekly objective that will get you to your goal.

Ask yourself one of the following on each of those New Year's Resolutions: What, How, Where, Why?

What do you consider "more money" and why do you need it? Maybe your objective isn't to become rich, but to have enough dough to buy a new car.

Why do you need a house? Why not a condo or an apartment?

Where do you want to go on vacation? There's a difference between planning a trip to Cairo and taking a jet to the Magic Kingdom. For that matter, why Cairo? Why not Petra? Why not Athens?

Why do you want to get pregnant? Do you really want a kid, or is it simply because all your friends have gotten into that craze?

Once you have that sorted out, only then can you truly apply the SMART protocol and start to make some headway into actively and dynamically obtaining your heart's desire.

Let's take this book as a perfect example of a SMART Goal achieved.

S - I want to write a book that outlines how successful people achieve their goals. I'll do this by making an outline and grouping all the data I have acquired throughout the years.

M - I will write a book. I want it ready by Summer 2020. Why? I don't really know but Summer seems like the perfect time for a launch. That gives me about eight months, as I have all of the research ready.

A - I will write and publish the book by July 2020. Who will write it? Well, me. I'll get some help along the way associated with publishing a book, and lock in a good editor.

R - If I put in 10-20 hours per week, the goal will be achieved. I need about 5,000 words per week to achieve this. Just checked online and the average writer can churn out about 7,000- 9,000 words a day…5k doesn't sound so outlandish.

T - Summer is the deadline. That's when it has to be ready. I'll need an outline, and I'll build from there.

7
THE YODA MODEL

"The mind is not a vessel to be filled, but a fire to be kindled."

Plutarch

L et's talk about Joseph Campbell, a man who quoted from Sinclair Lewis' novel *Babbitt* on a daily basis: *"Remember the last line?"* he'd ask a student or friend. *"'I have never done a thing that I wanted to do in my life.' That is a man who never followed his bliss."* There's a reason why Campbell died happy and content in Honolulu, Hawaii after a Grateful Dead concert...a concert he later wrote a conference on: *"Ritual and Rapture from Dionysus to the Grateful Dead."*

Well, back to the program. Campbell is an American legend. He's a historian, lecturer, and mythologist, and perhaps one of the most influential academics in the last century in the art of storytelling.

Campbell was a professor of literature at Sarah Lawrence College, with his studies having been in comparative mythology and comparative religion. That last bit is merely to emphasize that the man knew his stuff; he could hold his own in a dinner conversation. In 1949, Campbell, after exhaustive studies, published a work that would end up influencing the likes of Alan Watts, Jim Morrison and George Lucas, a work that would be taught at every university and film school from that point forward, his book: *The Hero with a Thousand Faces*.

The Monomyth

Campbell's concept in *The Hero with a Thousand Faces* refers to the monolith (ONE MYTH). It is an over-simplified theory that says that all mythic narratives are nothing more than variations of a single great story. The whole theory is based on the observation that most story arcs follow a common pattern regardless of their origins.

Campbell called this pattern, *"The Hero's Journey"*. The idea was so revolutionary that it not only made people in Hollywood and novelists do doubletakes, but psychologists reexamine the way such a primitive model might have influenced our psyche.
Why our psyche?

Because we are basically byproducts of all we observe. Of all the patterns we digest unconsciously. We collectively adhere to trends and traditional ways mainly because it comes naturally to us. Why does it come naturally? On account that it's everywhere in our lives. We believe in romantic love because Hollywood has installed that idea in our brain through countless repetitions. We believe in our "true selves" because Disney has told us that Aladdin, Simba, Mulan, Quasimode, Hercules, Ariel, Tony Stark, Stephen Strange, Woody, Buzz, and all the others finally managed to surpass their struggles when they discovered their "authentic selves"...when they uncovered "the diamond in the rough."

Now, for a second, imagine that there was this underlying theme or platform, this ONE MYTH, and that everything we've been told has accidentally followed that pattern. Psychologically speaking, it would be a game changer.

Well, to a degree, that was what Campbell proposed and in part proved. His theory is based on the idea that every story - even biographies, because they are filtered through writers and aren't real representations of what truly happened, just subjective interpretations - follows the same rules at a primitive level. At its core values, every story is identical.

Campbell's Hero's Journey is broken up into stages. While we are not going to go into great detail on each one (it's confusing), we are nonetheless going to mention them. Mind you, they are metaphorical stages and have an artistic flourish to their name.

It all starts when the hero decides to leave the KNOWN for the UNKNOWN.

- **Call to Adventure:** The hero or the individual feels he needs a change. They either have an inner calling, caused by some psychological key turn or turmoil, or they get an actual physical calling: "Knock, knock, this is Hagrid."
- **The Refusal to the Call:** The hero refuses the call, oftentimes out of a sense of duty or obligation, fear, insecurity, sense of inadequacy, or simply because he doesn't want to get off the couch.
- **Supernatural Aid:** The hero feels that it is beyond his command to deny said calling. There's something pushing him forward. It's his FATE or destiny to answer that calling. Something takes the answer or lack of action away from him.
- **Threshold Guardian(s):** Someone or something forestalls the hero from starting his adventure. It's his first obstacle.
- **Meeting the Mentor:** Once the hero has committed to his quest, consciously or unconsciously, his guide will appear, magically or because the hero seeks them out.

Now, here's where I want to stop - mainly because we might get derailed if we continue with the whole crucible - and focus on that last point. As the hero progresses, with the guide's help, he is met with challenges, a revelation - which is often referred to a death/rebirth scenario - a transformation, a sacrifice, and finally a gift - many times knowledge or power. They return to the known having changed and with a new lease on life.

Meeting the Mentor

Grab that template up above and your favorite hero's origin and it fits…right?

Luke finds the droids, they ask for his help, he refuses 'cause he's just a farm boy, a ghost/hologram pops up and begs, he meets up with Obi Wan, he refuses again, the Empire kills his uncles.

Tony Stark is constantly feeling like he could do more, Pepper bugs him, Rhode bugs him, the media bugs him, his inner self bugs him, he refuses to give in 'cause he loves his lifestyle, he's hurt and miraculously saved by the old man from the cave, Yinsen, who becomes his mentor.

Too highbrow?

Bratty girl acts like a jerk, everyone hates her, she gets stuck in a time loop, she refuses to acknowledge the time loop, she dies every day killed by the same masked man, she meets a guy who tells her about Groundhog Day, he becomes her mentor, each time she dies she comes back with more knowledge, she atones for being an asshat, she goes back to normality. That's the plot of *Happy Dead Day*.

That same template and model repeats itself over and over again; Gandalf, Doctor Strange, Simba, Aladdin, Hercules, Katniss Everdeen, Harry Potter… The mentor is there, sometimes in disguise (the Genie), sometimes as the romantic lead (Gosling teaching Emma to follow her dream and vice-versa in

La La Land), and sometimes they are an actual teacher like Dumbledore. But the mentor is there.

And that template isn't just copied in tales of fiction but in real life.

Kobe had Michael Jordan; Bieber had Scooter Braun; Zuckerberg had Steve Jobs; Maya Angelou mentored Oprah Winfrey; Warren Buffet mentored Bill Gates; Stella Adler taught Marlon Brando and De Niro; J.J. Abrams was 16 when Steven Spielberg took his under his wing; Socrates mentored Plato and then Plato mentored Aristotle; Gandhi had Gopal Krishna Gokale. Clarence Lavant, a/k/a The Black Godfather, mentored a ton of people, ranging from Barack Obama to Jamie Foxx to Quincy Jones and even Kamala Harris.

And yes, we're going to fixate on mentoring for this chapter, but I want to really highlight the idea that Campbell's Journey - his monomyth - is applicable to each and every one of these real-life cases. Why? Because of our interpretation, the way we fix and tweak our narrative due to our biases. When we sit down and retell our stories, we frame them with the patterns we are most familiar with…the patterns of heroes. We do this at an atavistic level. We want to be heroes.

Just think about it. How many stories and autobiographies started with the main subject lamenting his station in life? Or - in the case where he, she, or they were born with all the riches of the world - melancholically telling themselves and the readers:

"I felt like there was more to life. I knew I had a destiny to uphold."

They have to face their fears of leaving the known, of facing either prejudice or criticism or even their unruly parents or a "Guardian," and then flinging themselves into "adventure"…there, they'll find their mentor. Hell, our college experience basically starts off as that. We leave the nest, fighting against our own inadequacies and emotional hiccups. We go into a new life, having perhaps sacrificed our boyfriend or girlfriend: *"Please stay. I beg you, we're meant to always be together."* Or our parents' desires: *"But why go out of state? There's a perfectly good community college down the road? Don't you love us?"* Or our financial officer: *"You don't have the assets for a student loan."* We enter our college, our crucible, and BOOM! Instantly we cling to a mentor…a classmate, a teacher, an advisor, our roommate.

The Mentor Mentality

All in all, we have what is called a mentorship complex. We need mentors, not just because they have something to gift us, but because they are part of our journey. Society has instructed us that in order to be Kobe, Mayer, the Rock, or Oprah, we require a Yoda. Some hurdles are too hard, some paths too thorny, so our inner Frodo begs for a Gandalf.

Successful people call this not-so-secret weapon - because the second they win the Oscar, they go onstage and praise this person's aid - coaches, sponsors, teachers, gurus, or boards of directors. Or, if you're into the New Age terminology, *"Life Coaches."*

And mentors meanwhile desire to be lifted into that lofty space. Why? Because, in a way, the monomyth repeats itself until *"the teacher becomes the master."*

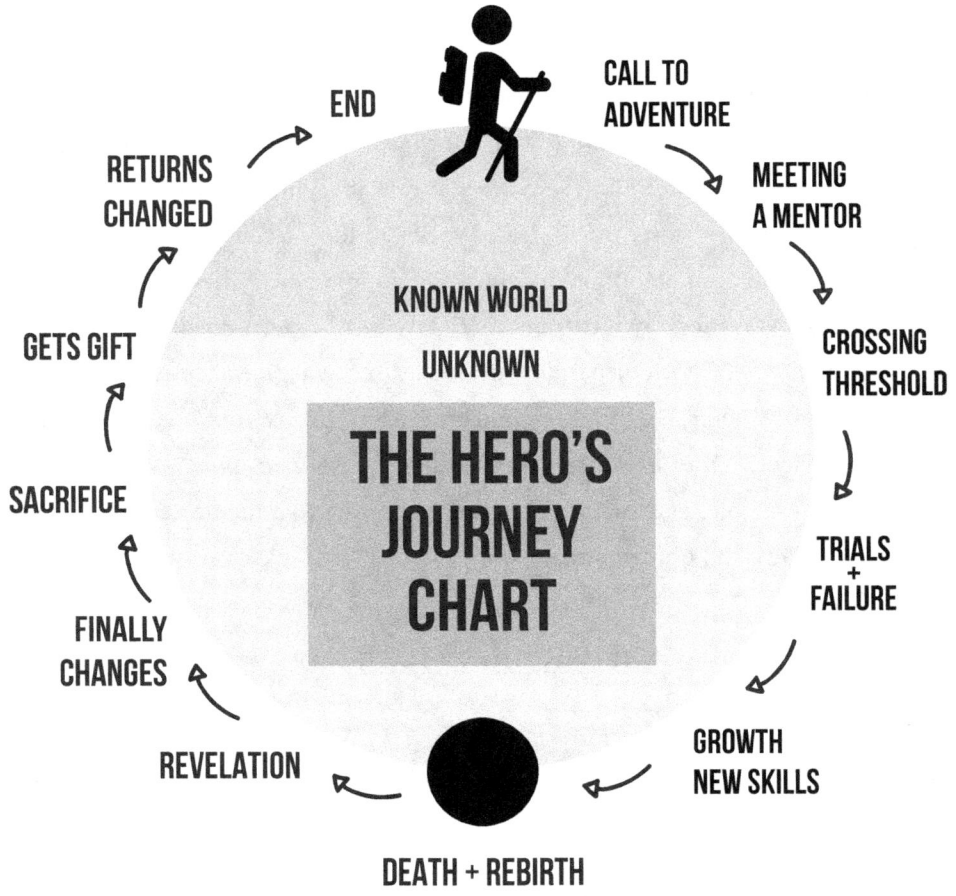

That's right, we aren't complete, the circle isn't closed until we've supplanted our mentor's place in the grand scheme of things. How do I know this? Well, I am writing a book based on what other people taught me so I can in turn teach you. That's right, I'm in fact replacing my mentors; this is an act of defiance. This book is me becoming Rocky to Apollo Creed's son.

It's part of our psyche, a psyche programmed by countless repetitions of the monomyth. Throughout time, this narrative structure has been in a loop, our minds bearing witness to the end of the myth. How does the myth truly end?

The mentor dies or retires. He becomes replaceable and slowly shifts into the background, forgoing the spotlight and handing it over to a new generation.

Obi Wan gets beaten by Vader and hands the journey over to Luke. Luke evaporates after he helps Rey out. Tony Stark becomes Peter Parker's guru, only to teach Spider-Man his greatest lesson by sacrificing himself to vanquish Thanos. Simba comes back to the pride, dislocates Scar from the throne, and takes his rightful place - where his dad once stood - and introduces his daughter to his subjects, the cycle starting anew. Sherlock becomes Watson's mentor, then plunges off the Richenbach Falls with his nemesis Moriarty. This cycle is something old and a routine that comes from our psyche; our need to supplant our parents. Sooner or later, our biological makeup demands that we take our lead as alpha of the pack. It is inevitable.

The Importance of a Mentor

A mentor teaches you not only what they know but where they screwed up along the way. They'll teach you all about the Force, but a couple of drinks in, they'll segue just as the Sith penetrated their order and banged them over the head. They'll try to frame their defeats and stumbles as moments of humility, but once you gain their trust, most members will tell you:

> *"Yes,* Indiana Jones 4 *was horrible. Everything about it was awful. I really don't know what I was thinking. It's was a career low point for me."*
>
> Steven Spielberg

Michael Jordan was departing the league when Kobe came in. He instantly saw the upstart and wanted to help. He taught Kobe how to score midrange. He taught Kobe about dominance in the field, how to expertly use jab steps, shimmies, and ball fakes. But above all, he told Kobe when to stop being an "arrogant ass" - his words, not mine. He taught Kobe the importance of humility and of teamwork.

Things to look for in a mentor:

- **Accessibility**: They have to be available. No half-hearted efforts. They'll meet up regularly (or virtually) and help you develop you objectives.
- **Authentic**: They must be genuinely interested in helping you. They are carbon copies of other mentors. They must have something unique that differentiates them from the pack.
- **Objectivity**: If you're out of touch and your idea sucks, they'll call you out on it. You want a mentor that shouldn't be your friend. You want someone who will be proactive, praise you when you deserve it, and bang you over the head with the truth when that's what you need.
- **Continual Learning**: Remember the foreword, "These are not our parents' times"? You need a mentor that's continually learning and a potential teacher who isn't stuck in their ways. Run for the hill if a mentor tells you, "That's the way it's always been done."
- **Values**: Your mentor's integrity should line up with yours. A mentor is someone you admire, someone you want to emulate, someone whom you should respect. Ask about their communication styles, their way of carrying themselves. They should never compromise their integrity more than you are willing to. Their values and believes, at a core level, should align.

Finding a Mentor

Throw a rock out the window, you'll hit one. Trust me. And if you live in the middle of the forest, where it's just you and your furry friends, then don't worry, because YouTube, podcasts, and Amazon have outsourced the need for a one on one. The internet is full of mentors, videos and teachings, forums, and so much more. You want to learn about video games...well, there's a Masterclass by the fellow who created the SIMS. Playing the guitar and starting a band? You have John Fogerty and another Masterclass by the Beastie Boys. Cooking? Gordon Ramsay. Writing historical fiction? Dan Brown.

They are on Facebook, Instagram, YouTube, Snapchat, next door, in your school, on LinkedIn...basically everywhere.

Friends & Family

"You are the average of the 5 people who you spend the most time with."

Jim Rohn,
American author, entrepreneur and motivational speaker

When you think of mentors, you instantly think of a sage with a grey beard, or the Kung Fu master that talks in Confucius riddles... You hardly envision your crazy hippie uncle who, at age 24, went on a five-year sabbatical through India and the Middle East.

The reality of the situation is that we are constantly being swamped by would-be mentors and teachers, fountains of wisdom and knowledge that have an orgasmic need to divulge their revelations – we just have to pick up on them. We have to focus on the fact that they exist.

Support groups, friends, family members, and your actual teachers are in fact paragons of success waiting to be tapped on their shoulder and asked:

"Spill it, what's your secret?"

That crazy uncle somehow financially supported a five-year trek through exotic lands, logistically planned it, and came back with bags full of insight and trinkets; he is a success story waiting to be interviewed. Why? Because you most likely need a one-year notice and detailed plan, not to mention thousands of apps, in order to map out a two-week holiday at an all-inclusive in Cancun. That uncle did all of that before TripAdvisor, Google Maps, YouTube How-To videos, and credit cards. He had to use actual paper maps, work out conversion rates, and call hostels in advance to figure out it they had a bed for the night. That person has a few things to teach you.

Look around, make a list, and determine not only who is successful - who's making a killing in their life - but who actually has something important to impart. Success is a vague, esoteric term, a shifting value that changes from one person to another, and based on what WE define as success. WE might encapsulate the concept as "being rich." WE might delineate it as a sense of happiness and peace. WE might interpret it as being able to charm and spellbind the opposite sex. Our definition is different from the person sitting right next to you or, for that matter, me, your writer. Success is something open to private interpretations - we each grant it a subjective worth. Our meaning of success differs from your uncle's or your parents' or your teachers'...BUT here's the thing – that doesn't mean that they have not obtained success within their own personal framework.

So, once more, look around and ask yourself:

> *"Who do I know that's successful? Not by what I define success, but by what they construe it as?"*

Lamas in Nepal[8] might not be rich, but they work tirelessly in their monastic lifestyles to be the best and obtain nirvana...to obtain the ultimate theological triumph possible. Grasp the sacred in their life. For a person who sees success as a Mercedes Benz and a nine-figure bank account, those recluses might seem weird, but does that mean that they, in their pious and humble lives, devoid of the pressures of capitalism, are less successful by comparison?

So ask yourself once more:

> *"Who do I know that's successful? Not by what I define success, but by what they construe it as?...AND HOW CAN I LEARN FROM THEM?"*

---

[8] Lama is a title for a teacher of the Dharma in Tibetan Buddhism. The name is similar to the Sanskrit term *guru*, meaning "heavy one," endowed with qualities the student will eventually embody. The Tibetan word "Lama" means "highest principle," and less literally "highest mother" or "highest parent" to show the close relationship between teacher and student.

8
BRINGING IT ALL TOGETHER

Between a Rock & a Hard Place

Dwayne Johnson: the name along brings a smile to your face. He's one of the most charismatic and successful actors in Hollywood as of 2020.

"I'd vote for the Rock. The Rock for President of the United States."

A poll conducted by Newsweek on likability of 2016 presidential candidates; Trump and Clinton didn't even break the 20-point glass ceiling, The Rock was a fill-in name that started getting traction.

Dwayne Douglas Johnson was born on May 2, 1972. He's an American-Canadian actor, producer, retired professional wrestler, former professional football player, businessman, and all-around cool guy. He is considered one of the highest-grossing box office stars of all time; his films have grossed over 10.5 billion dollars worldwide.

Johnson started his career as a college football player for the University of Miami, winning the national championship in 1991. Right from that period, Johnson discovered that he had a knack for sports and, above all, for reinventing himself. In the span of five years, the Rock - as he would later be called - switched from college football to draft member of the Calgary Stampeders of the Canadian Football League (CFL). In 1996, Johnson secured a contract with the World Wrestling Federation (WWF). Very quickly, Johnson rose to province after developing a charismatic, boastful, and trash-talking persona known as the Rock. During his time in the league, the Rock was considered one of the greatest professional wrestlers and biggest draws of all time. He was the cash cow.

Then, in 2001, Johnson said to himself:

"I can make it on the silver screen."

With that thought, Johnson decided to move to Hollywood and begin his acting career. But how did a wrestling superstar become one of the biggest names in the movie industry?

Let's crunch the numbers

By this point, after so many years of getting to know himself, the Rock had all his self-concepts down to an art form. He knew what made him tick, what pissed him off, what inspired him, what psychological baggage he was carrying. The Rock had therapists giving him professional advice and analysis; he had his concepts of who he was sealed tight.

The Rock knew that his acting chops were lacking, to put it mildly. He knew he couldn't coast on his looks, his muscles, and his charisma. Up until then, all Dwayne knew about acting was that when in doubt, break a wooden chair over your scene partner's head…a tactic that wouldn't fly with Robert De Niro.

He was also aware that, for all intents and purposes, he was starting in a completely new world, one dominated by egos, academics, and masters. A world built on legends. Yes, Dwayne came from a world of larger-than-life figures, but figures whose shine wasn't timeless…figures and stars that eventually faded into obscurity. Figures that were famous in a niche. Now, Johnson had to trade jabs with Stallone, De Niro, DiCaprio. He had to take directions, perfectly choreographed directions from world-renowned directors. He had to understand the magic of special effects and how everything worked on a movie set.

Also, the Rock was aware that his gruff, boisterous attitude - although charming in the ring - might be a bit off-putting during a table read. He was also working against a stereotype: "The big muscle bound jock without a brain."

The first thing that The Rock did was alter his habits, rituals and routines. Yes, he continued to work on his body, on his fallback career and all that entailed but, he also started to take acting classes, movie classes, he started to frequent directorial workshops, he started to pick the brain of people who were in the biz. He made it his objective to mine the outskirts of Hollywood and bone up on the workings of this town.

During this period, he started to see an opportunity. Most of the big-name action stars - the blockbuster/headliners - were growing old and stale. Stallone, Willis, and Schwarzenegger were no longer running the show. Mel Gibson was becoming a caricature of himself and Hollywood was desperate for new blood. The iron was hot and somebody needed to strike it.

Dwayne started to learn all he could about the finance of Hollywood, the mechanics of making a movie, and the patterns of what made it tick. Yes, he wanted to be an actor, but that didn't stop him from learning about quarterly reports, or why one lens was better than the other, or what it takes to get a pith off the ground and into pre-production.

Johnson understood, above all, that he needed to start at the bottom. He worked his way into the boardrooms and meetings by starring in music videos, then appearing in *That 70s Show* and *Star Trek*. He worked the rounds and did everything in order to get his IMBD[9] page some entries. Then, in 2001, enter *The Mummy Returns*. *The Mummy* was the Rock's big break - if you could call it a break. In the film, he barely spoke and only appeared in the beginning and at the climax; in the latter as a badly rendered CGI monstrosity, a bare-chested, ponytail-wearing man whose lower body constituted of scorpion legs and a

[9] International Movie Data Base

black stinger. But here's the thing, why did the Rock submit himself to such a showcase of depravity? Because, due to his knowledge of "movie law" - that's the term I'm going to bundle the intricacy of Hollywood under - he managed to tack onto his contract the starting role in a Mummy spin-off: *The Scorpion King*.

It took the Rock more than 10 years to actually attain the level he craved as a Hollywood powerhouse. His strategy? Put in the work and hack the system. How did he hack the system? Simply put, he gave them bang for their buck. He was a charismatic actor who always showed up on set on time, was a consummated professional with incredible people skills, and was cheap compared to his peers. Plus, more importantly, the Rock knew that no role was too small. He began fostering relationships and, above all, acting across the board: family-friendly films, action set pieces, comedies, dramas.

The Rock had a goal and he did everything to meet that goal. He became a social media celeb when the term was in its infancy. He wined and dined with diplomats. He ate tacos off food trucks with his old Floridian friends. He cracked open a beer or two with Kevin Hart.

He has been named as one of the most influential people of the world – twice! And his Instagram account is currently listed as the fourth most viewed on that platform.

A Writer's Workshop

I'm going to dig into each and every chapter and give you an overall overview of how I composed and brought this thing to life.
Above everything, throughout every step, what drove me was a desire; the idea of actually fulfilling a dream and an objective. Of stepping outside my comfort

zone, my wheelhouse, and in fact putting my suppositions and theories to the test. This book is as much for you as it is for me.

Self-Concept:

- I had to dig really deep and learn what I was good at. I'm good at making really complex concepts and strategies easy for the average Joe to understand. I learned that I have a network that is representative from so many backgrounds. CEOs, Gardeners, DJs, Sales Managers, Promoters, Therapists, Small Business Owners, Teachers, Coaches, Nurses, Students, and the list goes on. People from tech, entrepreneurship, entertainment, healthcare, and so forth. I knew that I had to write something that would benefit all of them, not just one group.
- I knew that a book would be the best format because I could iterate multiple times before publishing and clearly outline my thoughts. Also, it's tangible. I can go to a high school in south central LA and give an amazing talk and inspire students, but to be able to give them something they can hold that outlines strategies that they can implement that day – that's what I wanted. And a book is the best format.
- I also had to understand that this was my first foray into the whole swamp that is making a book. I had to lean into that and try to create a framework of what I was going to experience. Like I said, I cannot alter the past, but maybe in altering or, at the very least, coming to terms with my Present-Self, I could create a book I would ultimately be proud of.
- There was a lot of soul-searching involved, a great deal of research and self-doubt and, above all, fear…times that I felt like I was making a fool of myself.

My Habits/Rituals/Routines

- Made it a habit to write very single day.
- Made it a habit to continue learning via podcasts, books, interviews, every single day, 7x a week.
- Read Stephen King's fantastic book, *On Writing: A Memoir of the Craft*.
- Read books that didn't interest me. Books that at face value seemed awfully dull but as time passed and I digested them, I understood their value. *Sapiens: A Brief History of Humankind* was one of them.
- I kept my habit of working out 6-7x a week because it provided me with the clarity and energy to keep writing, even after a 10-hour workday at Snapchat. Working out, forgoing the troubles of the mind, helped me out. Later, I realized that it was as close to meditation as I was able to achieve. It kept me grounded.
- Kept my rituals in place and set a ton of limits - did not go out much, did not watch or listen to any TV, Netflix, radio, news, etc. Removed as many distractions as possible, the general idea being that distractions are the mother of procrastination.

Compound Learning

- Even while writing the book, I was still stress-testing the framework by continuing to listen to interviews, talk to people, watch documentaries, read autobiographies and books, etc. I was always learning and picking up on things that I learned in order to apply them to the book. I even applied these principles that I outlined in the book in order to learn more. Learned from support groups and friends. Learned from people online. Learned from watching industry leaders from afar. Learned from people at work and how they phrase things, present themselves. I learned from friends who are sales managers, which will help me in a few months when I'm selling the book. I learned from my marketing friends as I wrote the marketing strategy. I learned from my family and friends and how they consume content — also, what content would be most relevant to include in the book and how to present it. I learned nonstop not only for the information that would be in the book, but how I would present to a room, how I would sell the book, how I would market the book, how I could make it go viral by learning from YouTubers or other famous people, learning from people who are great at social media like Will Smith, and thinking about how I could implement some of his video tactics into my marketing strategy to promote the book. I learned from my DJ and nightlife friends and how they promote parties/shows and how I could use some of these strategies to promote the book. So many other examples too — but I always had an eye and ear out to pick up on things in my daily life that would help me with the book.

Deliberate Work/Putting in the Work

- You really can't rush a book creation process. It took about a year to pull together all of the stories, research, and organize everything. Once I started writing, it was putting in 15-20 hours a week to create the outline and 50-page brain dump before bringing in an editor to help. Once working with my editor, it still required 15 hours a week to write, review, edit, expand, etc. — the entire process of writing the book took 8-9 months. You can't speed it up and there's no way around it. Gotta put in the work and work deliberately. No distractions, full concentration, tons of coffee, a great pair of headphones, and a few beers here and there in Arts District LA.

- <u>Hacks</u>: Learned and started cherishing thousands of different apps, software and technological wonders that really helped in tightening my phrases and building my rhetoric…and cleaning up my grammar. Apps like Hemingway, Grammarly, Readability, Clearscope.
- For the first time in my life, I downloaded a Thesaurus into my phone. That was a turning point.
- Created a bizarre array of screens – my own mission control. My laptop always on and the newest draft of the book opened, my chrome browser with tabs upon tabs of research, my phone/thesaurus at hand.

Self-Talk, Affirmations, Driving Forces, Ego

- Even with the support of an editor, this was the most difficult thing I've ever done in my life. By far. There were a ton of times where I just thought that I wasn't going to be able to pull it off and I was way over my head with the project, but too late to turn back, as I'd put it out in the world. And I always complete my projects.
- I had to use self-talk and affirmations and tap into my ego throughout the entire process. I would tell myself, "If I don't do this, then I don't know if anyone else will. And people deserve to learn what I've learned in order to achieve their goals. We need more great Latino authors in the world to represent for underrepresented groups." This definitely feeds the ego, but it helped because it also provided my "why" – the ego put me into overdrive in order to complete the project.

Goal-Setting, Goal-Executing

- Created a very detailed project plan with milestones and things to complete. The goal was summer 2020 and we are on track to meet it (even ahead of schedule by a couple of weeks).
- I checked the project plan every time I worked on the book...so pretty much every day.
- Crafted a goal-oriented structure for the book...halfway through it, started working on instinct.

Friends, Supporting Groups, Mentors

- Before announcing the book, I told my close group of friends and loved ones about it, which held me accountable to keep it going. Also served as a good group of people to bounce ideas off, as they all fall within the target audience that I was trying to reach most.
- Joined about 10 online groups across Facebook, LinkedIn, text, and Instagram. All of these include other authors and entrepreneurs, which kept me motivated and helped me learn from during the creation process.
- Got the help of about five different mentors, all with different strengths, to guide me in the right direction for things like marketing strategy, book launch (two of them being previously written books that performed really well); these people also served as a sounding board for ideas and feedback throughout the process.
- Coach: Well, less of a coach but hired a beast editor that helped with a ton of areas in which I lacked the expertise. As I mentioned, I have never been strong when it comes to writing, but I do have good ideas and am good at picking up on themes, as well as consolidating really complex and abstract

strategies for the normal person to understand. My editor, Max Longstone, helped a ton with unraveling the story, copying, and bringing the book to life. Thank you, Max. I really couldn't have done this without you and I truly appreciate you sticking it through with me. I know I can be handful and you did a phenomenal job the entire time. Especially with my flood of questions, constant feedback, and ridiculous amount of messages via WhatsApp whenever I found a new piece of data that I felt we needed to squeeze into the book. It has been a ton of fun working with you and I'm already chipping away at the next book. So let's celebrate after the launch and get back to the grind.[10]

Chaos

- Magic: After a while, the project gets wings and you start to feel as if you've lost control of it and it has obtained a life of its own. All projects are like that. You start to see angles and opportunities you never knew existed. You start to instinctually comprehend that the project isn't just a collection of moving parts but that it has a soul. Stephen King once said that starting a book was like rowing a boat into the middle of the ocean and getting lost; after weeks, you either see a shoreline or you get swept by the current. It's a bit like that, when you finally see the shoreline, in many cases - mine included - you bear witness to a landscape you had never envisioned; the end result is wonderful and at the same time completely different from what you had thought of. In my case, I realized that the book needed infographics, design, images, and color - so a huge thanks to Johanna Pizlo for making this happen. They came out amazing! I also realized that it needed chapters, like the foreword and

---

[10] Letter from Max… "Ish, I had a blast. It was fun. It was hair-raising. It was challenging… But more importantly, it was a hoot. Stop making me blush, you got this. You did the heavy lifting."

afterword, which I hadn't taken into account. I came to the startling, eye-opening certainty that the text needed a bit more of "Me"…the first draft was "KOBE SQUARE."

- Outside influences: I created this book while partly locked down by COVID-19… It is in many cases a child of that era. I started it before the Coronavirus outbreak and finished it during it. I don't know in what way that influenced me and the text. I'm not certain whether it allowed me to focus more and ignore distractions, but I'm sure it somehow influenced this book.
- Kobe: During the writing of this book, Kobe perished in a fatal helicopter ride. I think it's important to acknowledge it. It's important to understand that while I was writing about him, while I was being inspired by him, while I was following in his footsteps, Kobe died. I dedicated this book to my parents and family, but part of it was written with Kobe in mind; he was a force in my world view.

The Hypothetical Hippodrome

I actually have no idea what that headline actually means…I just thought it sounded cool. Aren't alliterations cool?

So far we've explored how the Rock and other big shots accomplished their goals. We've also digested some examples of how someone without their bank accounts and lifestyles might be able to obtain similar prizes. Why do I make emphasis on the dollars to doughnut weight they lug around? Because of a simple principle. What's Batman's real power? That he's rich!

It's easy to trust in each and every one of you, and tell you that in spite of your setbacks, you too can reach, at the drop of a hat, the momentous peaks of triumph as someone like Obama and Johnson. To collect everyone into the same duffle bag. But the truth is that for us regular Joes, those lofty heights are a bit harder to reach without the private helicopter so readily available to the likes of Steve Jobs.

So, given that incredibly discouraging reality, I've decided to bring our final example of how to mash all the teachings in this books together and actually bring the Gold Olympic rings of success down to Earth.

How many of you have gone up to a mirror and said:

"I need a better job."

It's simple, relatable, and universal. You're stuck behind a cubicle getting a "sunburn" from those depressing halogen lamps. You're coming home overnight smelling of fried chicken. You're barely making a dent on your credit card bill. You're cemented into the same dull routine constantly watching your life go by.

The reality is that your job, given the effort and time you sacrifice to it, is an intricate part of your makeup. We are, to a degree, our workstation. So, unless you're jumping for joy at the prospect of going to work, there's a good chance that each day you clock in, you're swamped by the nagging thought that you need to hit the road and find a better job.

This is going to be the ground on which we will build our church. The example, engaging and approachable to all, on which we will swing everything we've learned from this book and see if all those theories past the smell test.

First of all, WHAT'S THE GOAL?

"I need a better job."

What exactly did we learn in Chapter 6?
"S.M.A.R.T.! That's right, you've been paying attention."

It's incurably vague, that phrase and that goal. We need to whittle it down and personalize it. So ask yourself, what does the word *"better"* actually pertain to? What is a *"better job"* for you?

- Is it one where you earn more money?
- Is it one where you can come home to your family at an earlier time?
- Is it one that's not as physically demanding?
- Is it one that has a different set of folks as team members or work colleagues?
- Is it one that applies to what you studied in school?
- Is it one where you are more in tune with nature and you have more outdoor time?
- Is it one that's closer to home?
- Is it one that relates to your passions and hobbies?
- Is it one where travel is involved?
- Is it your same job, only with a promotion?
- Is it one with better medical benefits?
- Or maybe you simply don't want to work anymore?

Lock down what a better job actually entails. It's something unique and wholly singular to your needs; it's something intimate and partly drawn up by your psyche. The need, the goal, and its interpretations change from person to person.

Once you have that, quantify the adjective or the verb; give it something by which you can measure it.

- At what time do you want to arrive home?
- How closer to your home - in miles - do you want your job to be?
- Where do you want to travel? Or how often do you want to travel?
- What promotion or position are you hungry for?
- What medical benefits do you want?
- How much more money do you want to earn?
- What are you looking for in your new work buddies?
- What fields does your diploma adhere to?
- What are the skills that you want to flex in your job?

It's all about focusing and breaking it down. Diminishing the borders and making it more tangible. It's no longer simply an imaginative goal or objective that's slippery and incredibly farfetched, but something you can actually see as obtainable.

For example:

> "I want a job that allows me at least two more hours of playtime with my kids."

That above opens a wealth of possibilities, of ways to obtain that goal.

- Do you need to commute closer? Can you find a job that's closer to home?
- Can you change your timesheet?
- Can you work from home?
- Why do you need two hours? Quantity over quality?
- Is this something you feel you need or something that's being asked of you?
- Do you need to change jobs? If so, what's available?
- Can you cut-back on your hours at your work?

Now, before you go to your boss and demand that he give you a new laptop and high-speed internet (that way, you can create your own little command center from home and work directly from there), you have to understand who you are.

That's right, Chapter 1.

Define your self-concepts. Ask yourself all the tricky questions.

- Do I even like to travel?
- Do I even like my kids?
- Okay, sure, I don't want to work…I want to invest and let my money do the hard work. How adept am I in with the whole trading fiasco? Do I even have seed money?
- Can I really focus working straight from my house?
- Why do I even need those medical benefits?

If you're certain of the sort of person you are, these and a dozen other questions will be incredibly simple to answer. If, on the other hand, you've never once stopped to analyze the sort of person emotionally, psychologically, and physically that you've turned into…then you have a long way to go before even attempting to fulfill a life-altering mission.

But, let's say you've gotten this far.

You discover that you need regulations and someone to actually control you during your work days. Why? Because it seems you have a flighty mind and aren't exactly efficient without a diligent taskmaster cracking their whip over your shoulder.
You feel the need to be with your kids. It's not an imposition and your better half isn't forcing you to make that decision; you simply have a paternal/maternal desire to spend more time with them. *"They're growing up so fast."*

You also discover that your finances can't take the hit of working fewer hours.

And, during this introspection, it pops up that you hate, I mean HATE, getting up too early. You already set your alarm at 6:30 AM and half the time, you're sleeping on the job.

- Do you need to commute closer? Find a job that's closer to home?
- ~~Can you change your timesheet?~~
- ~~Why do you need 2 hours? Quantity over quality?~~
- ~~Is this something you feel you need or something that's being asked of you?~~
- ~~Can you work from home?~~
- Do you need to change jobs? If so, what's available?
- ~~Can you cut-back on your hours at your work?~~

You start to break down your options and start assessing the ones that will actually work for you. That will ultimately make your mission a successful one.

You look at what's left from that list you compiled and decide: *"Fine I'll change jobs!"*

You hit up LinkedIn, Glassdoor, and all the other job sites out there and discover that the only jobs available that will actually fulfill your goal - getting at least two more hours with my kids - are outside your comfort zone. You have zero experience in the fields they touch.

Time to hit the books, podcasts, and free online classes and find mentors in that field. It's time to bulk up your lingo, your ego, and your C.V. It's time to change your habits and routines, put in the work, and get a teacher/guru; so many chapters, just check the Table of Contents.

You craft a realistic analysis of your resources and find them lacking. If you make a go at that goal right this very instant, right now, you're not going to make it. Why? Because you need skills and expertises that aren't in your wheelhouse.

Suddenly, to change jobs, you first have to change your interests. You first have to clear one goal in order to reach your primary objective. You went in thinking it was a short foot race, only to discover that it's a marathon. You created an algorithm.

In order to get the job you want, you first have to learn about X topic and become, if not proficient, at least knowledgable in that subject matter. Your initial ambition goes on the back burner. Your new intent and purpose of action is to transform your curriculum...and to understand, to put it bluntly, that when you do go into that office for that fateful interview, you're going to have to partly bullshit[11] your way into your dream job (Chapter 5: You Have One Hell Of An Ego). You'll have to sell yourself and make up for your lack of experience with grit and bravado; you'll have to put on a show.

So let's see how *"I need a better job"* was molded by the lessons I taught you. Let's read what that five-letter edict turned into.

> *"I need to get X job that allows me to hit my driveway two hours earlier than my current position so I can be with my kids. In order to get that job, I need to learn all I can about Y subject. In order to learn all I can and actually have an opportunity at that position, I will need to read Z books, take Z classes, and have sit-downs with Z teachers I found online. In order to do all of that, I need to change my schedule, allocate at least three hours a day for studying, change my weekly calendar – damn, no more clubbing with my friends - for about four months. Once I get proficient enough, I'll have to partly wing it in the interview; BE CONFIDENT!"*

Now you have an actual timetable and recipe. You have a cheatsheet on how to obtain your goal; an algorithm.

---

[11] Pardon the French.

Afterword
What It All Means

We're at the tail-end of our journey and nearing the finishing line. This is usually the part where the author - that's me, by the way - wraps everything up in a neat little bow and leaves you with some parting words, the final advice... Well, as a first time writer, who am I to defy the norms? Let's give the audience what they paid for.

If I follow the guidelines properly, then right now, I have no other choice but to pluck an anecdote from my time stream, lay it out before you, and dissect it in order to handsomely escort you toward that last nugget of wisdom. That final advice or tip that closes the book and blanket wraps, all warm and fuzzy inside. Well, I have a question for you: Aren't you sick and tired of getting to know me? Let's be honest, by now I've swapped more tales and stories and insights about myself than with my girlfriend. You and I have gotten, well, too intimate.

So, with that said, and frankly, because I'm running out of yarns to spin, I'm going to yank out of the limelight someone we can all relate to...Deadpool. If we're going to end this book, it might as well be with a great cameo, awesome production values, and with the proverbial bang. Yes, Hugh Jackman was busy.

Anyway, Deadpool (or Ryan Reynolds) was born in Canada on October 23, 1976. The man was enamored of action and he started out his gymnastics trial for the gold ring of celebrity at a very early age. His first break was in a Canadian teen soap opera. Ryan was hip, Ryan was funny, Ryan was handsome,

Ryan had all the makings of future Hollywood star; the kid was charming and well liked. From 1991-1993, he starred in the soap opera *Hillside* and, after production was shut down, he was flushed from one minor role to another. He was kicked around, everyone amazed that he simply wasn't making it. One flop after another. His first partial hit was in 2009, and he wasn't even the main actor of the film - *X-Men Origins: Wolverine*. *Deadpool*, the movie that finally put him on the Hollywood hotlist, was released in 2016, and the studios were so unimpressed by the cut they had seen of the film that they basically shoved the end-product into a fatal funnel: Valentine weekend, a notoriously lazy period for superhero movies. This was, to many in the industry, Ryan's final gamble. Everyone thought that the movie would be a bomb or, at most, an underground hit and cult favorite.

Ryan even partly financed the film with the last bit of his cash. He was putting everything on the line. He became the creative director of *Deadpool*'s unconventional marketing campaign. The movie, as you know, unless you've been living under a rock, became a financial and critical success, breaking multiple records and earning over 782 million dollars against a 58-million-dollar budget.

So, Ryan started to work as an actor in 1990 and he finally scored a hit in 2016…a 26-year-long struggle. Sure, he had multiple roles in all types of movies but he was making ends meet. The male lead to Sandra Bullock, the comedic underpin to Snipes' Blade, the "Let's never talk about it disaster" that was *Green Lantern*. For over 26 years Ryan starred in almost everything that was put before him. Every movie role. Every tiny part. Every guest star. Every two-bit series. He almost never turned a role down, no matter how small or outside his range. Why? Two reasons. One, Ryan had to eat. Two, Ryan had a dream. He wanted to be a household name and he wanted to finally land a part that would catapult him into stardom.

Now, Ryan Reynolds is not only one of the most profitable actors in the industry, with perhaps the biggest bang for his buck in returns, but he's also one of the most well-liked celebrities out there; not to mention that he was married to Scarlett Johansson and now Blake Lively. During that 26-year climb, he not only graduated as a star but also as a savvy venture capitalist and entrepreneur - owner of Aviation American Gin, as well as Mint Mobile Communications. He's also an incredibly adept social media user, as well as a marketing powerhouse – the man spearheading publicity junkets and the creative strategies of all his brands.

26 years. Not two, not one, but 26 years. And Ryan isn't the only one; Hollywood is plagued by celebrities that didn't give up on their dreams and only managed success years after they had taken their first tentative steps into the arena. Christoph Waltz was 51 when Tarantino finally came knocking at his door. Alan Rickman had been a struggling theater actor, he was 46 when Bruce Willis shoved him out the Nakatomi Towers in *Die Hard*. Bruce Willis was at his rope's end because his TV series was ending and every time he tried his hands at a movie, the film would crash and burn. Bryan "Walter White" Cranston, 44. Lucille Ball, 40. Sean Connery had been working since he was a kid and only landed the James Bond role at 32.

And it's not just actors, but almost everyone who had to break into any industry without any sort of help had to grind the pavement and really put in the elbow grease. Lady Gaga began her career almost right out of the womb. Sure, Poker Face Gaga was 20 when she scored her first hit, but she was grooming herself since the tender age of seven. Steve Jobs, as we've discussed, had thousands of downfalls and thousand of hits…he was constantly reinventing himself. There's a reason why most politicians seem like they are just a couple of years from being hit by their own tombstones, why - aside from a few renowned cases - most look like they live in a pickle jar and only come out for public appearances. It takes a long time to actually become a senator or congressman, or even the President, if you don't belong to a clique or one of those funky Skull Societies.

It takes work and the will to believe that you're living for your dream…not that it's dragging you down. Marc Maron, one of the best stand-up comedians in the industry, once said:

> *"There were times that I felt that more than a dream it was an anchor. It took me years to actually get any traction in my career, half my performances were in dingy empty theaters - me playing to one guy… But it takes work, and sweat, and disappointment. You have to become best friends with depression and frustration. Self doubt is your cocaine buddy. It takes time to master playing Marc Maron."*

That's really the final advice I have to give. If you take anything from this book it should be that… **IT TAKES TIME, IT TAKES WORK.**

The one quality, above all, that successful people have, the one thing they all have in common…the ability to believe that they are going to make it.

They never give up.

They never back down.

They always work tirelessly for their dream.

They build their reality, and fight for it until fate, destiny, or reality itself bends to their will.

They take hit after hit, get up, and keep going…

Some win by exhausting everyone else.

Successful people are pigheaded, stubborn, mulish, and headstrong; they never yield. During their low moments, they may live above their parents' garage, sleep on a friend's couch for a few months, or in a dorm room until they are kicked out for being "too old," squatting on the streets, pinching every penny for a meal, but they never give up. They become frustrated, they contemplate following their old man's advice and "getting a decent job," they bitch and scream about being stuck in the same place.

And every day, they sing under their breath:

> *"Dedication, hard work, plus patience."*
> Nipsey Hussle, American rapper

'Cause it's not going to be easy. Not one bit. But it's worth every second.

And lastly, remember this one thing.

They truly define what success means to them.

They don't let anyone else dictate it.

Now that you've got the framework to achieve your goals, it's time to get shit done.

Let's get it, y'all.

A Note from the Author

Someone recently asked me what differentiates my book from the thousands of other self-development books out there. My response:

"The audience."

I wrote the book with a diverse audience in mind. I wrote it for an audience that is often neglected, overlooked, and underrepresented. I read 45 self-development books last year. Three of them were written by people of color. None of them happened to be Latino.

I believe that more people deserve the knowledge and resources to achieve their goals. I think there's something special about being able to connect with the person who you're learning from. Being able to relate to that person, their references, examples, and culture.

By writing this book, I want to show people from underrepresented groups that it is possible to achieve their goals, even when there may not be people who look like them, talk like them, or come from similar backgrounds as they do.

I wrote this book for my people."

Cheers,

Ish Verduzco

www.ingramcontent.com/pod-product-compliance
Lightning Source LLC
Chambersburg PA
CBHW052349220526
45465CB00003BA/1023